People and Life 1

People and Life 1

Author Jack McBain
Publisher Chung Kyudo
Editors Kim Jinsuk, Cho Sangik, Kwak Bitna
Designers Park Bohee, Lee Seunghyun

First Published July 2017
By Darakwon Inc.
Darakwon Bldg., 211, Munbal-ro, Paju-si, Gyeonggi-do 10881
Republic of Korea

Tel. 82-2-736-2031 (Ext. 550)

ISBN 978-89-277-0933-6 14740
978-89-277-0932-9 14740 (set)

http://www.darakwon.co.kr

Main Book / Free MP3 Available Online
13 12 11 10 9 8 7 24 25 26 27 28

People and Life 1

Introduction

People and Life 1 is the first book in a four-level series for adult and young adult learners of English. This dynamic series contains material appropriate for students ranging from a beginning level to an intermediate level. Each book in the series provides more challenging material in order to meet the linguistic needs of a diverse community of language learners.

People and Life 1 has 12 units, each of which consists of a warm-up, 4 supporting lessons, and a wrap-up, which serves as a review of the unit. The book covers a variety of topics set in a Western sociocultural context. Students will find topics such as friends, food, and hobbies interesting and relevant. Topics that are accessible and relevant to a student's life make learning English easier and more fun.

As a multi-skill course book, *People and Life 1* introduces essential everyday English with speaking, listening, writing, reading, grammar, and vocabulary sections. However, the speaking and listening sections have been emphasized due to the critical importance of these two language skills. *People and Life 1* offers numerous opportunities for students to engage in conversations and participate in activities in English. Through these interactive, confidence-gaining, and interesting activities, students can develop their communication skills and make progress toward greater competence in English.

Author's Acknowledgments

The author would like to express his most sincere gratitude to the editor Ms. Jinsuk Kim. Without her tireless work and guidance, this project would not have been possible. He would also like to acknowledge the contributions of the Darakwon management and staff. Finally, he would like to extend a heartfelt thanks to his family, who have been incredibly patient during the writing process of this book.

Scope and Sequence

Unit	Learning Outcomes	Speaking
Unit 1 Introducing Myself p.11 My name is Maria Smith. I am from Mexico. What's your phone number? She's a chef.	***Students can . . .*** ask for and say names talk about where they are from ask for and say numbers talk about what people do	Introductions Nationalities Numbers and email addresses Business card Jobs Guessing famous people
Unit 2 My Family and Friends p.21 Do you have a sister? They are both kind! Who is this? People I Know	***Students can . . .*** ask and answer questions about their families ask and answer questions about age describe personalities and appearances	Family Appearances and personalities Colors Describing yourself to the class My best friend
Unit 3 Things p.31 What's in your bag? What is this? Which one is it? I am messy.	***Students can . . .*** identify common objects ask and answer questions about objects describe the locations of objects ask and answer questions about their rooms	Borrowing items Where things are Describing my room
Unit 4 Daily Life p.41 My show is on. I get up at 7 o'clock. How's your sister? I never take the bus.	***Students can . . .*** tell time and schedules talk about daily habits say ordinal numbers say how often they do something by using adverbs of frequency	Favorite TV show Telling time Typical Monday schedule Inviting someone to a party Survey: How often do you do . . . ?
Unit 5 Pastimes and Weekends p.51 What do you do on the weekend? What do you do for fun? What do you do on the weekend when it's sunny? My Day Off	***Students can . . .*** talk about weekend activities talk about hobbies and fun activities talk about activities they do in different weather and seasons describe a typical day off	Weekend schedule Bingo: Do you play . . . ? Activities you do for fun Activities for different seasons or events Robin's typical Saturday
Unit 6 Directions p.61 Where are you? / I live on Green Street. How do I get to the park? Around Town Popular Places to Visit	***Students can . . .*** describe where they are ask for and give directions to places understand directions and find places on maps talk about places in their cities	Giving directions Asking for directions Finding places on maps Asking about popular places in a person's city Survey: Most popular place in classmates' cities

Grammar	Listening	Vocabulary	Reading / Writing
Possessive adjectives	Introductions Where are they from? Numbers and email addresses	Titles Nationalities Numbers 0 to 10 Jobs	**Reading** *She's a chef.* **Writing** *My Favorite Celebrity*
Questions with *do* ~ *have* and *how old*	Jonathan's family Tim's friends	Numbers 11 to 100 Personalities and appearances More jobs Colors, clothes, and accessories	**Reading** Karen's family *People I Know* **Writing** Describing the woman in the picture *My Friends*
Singular and plural nouns Demonstrative pronouns *this, that, these, those* Prepositions of place	Pierre's desk In the room In front of a store	Items	**Reading** *I am messy.* **Writing** Messy people
Present simple tense Prepositions *in, on, at*	Times Birthday party	Telling time Ordinal numbers Adverbs of frequency	**Reading** Two people's typical days *I never take the bus.* **Writing** Typical days
Expressions about sports and activities *play, go –ing, do* *Wh-* questions *who, when, where* More about *when*	Caroline's day off What do you do for fun? Activities for weather and seasons	Weather and seasons	**Reading** *My Day Off* **Writing** What do your classmates do for fun? A typical day off
Prepositions of place	Place names Directions Find a person or shop on the map	How to give directions Places on a map	**Reading** Directions Finding places on maps An online post *Map of Fisherman's Wharf* **Writing** A popular place in a classmate's city

Grammar	Listening	Vocabulary	Reading / Writing
So and *too*	Prices Exchanging and returning items Favorite shops	Money Departments in a shopping mall	**Reading** *Shopping Habits* **Writing** Favorite shop
Some and *any*	What do we have in the fridge? What do we need to buy? Ordering food Le Café	Food items Measure words	**Reading** Mila's text messages *A Recipe for a Weekday Super Pizza* **Writing** *My Salad*
Present continuous tense Imperatives	Illnesses, symptoms, and advice A doctor's advice A man's healthy lifestyle	Common illnesses and symptoms Numbers of times	**Reading** *Old but Healthy* **Writing** How healthy are you?
Permission and ability of *can*	Benjamin's abilities An internship and a job interview A job application Practicing for an interview Opportunity abroad	Parts of a company	**Reading** *Is doing an internship good or bad?* *Looking for a job* *Opportunity Abroad* Volunteer ad **Writing** Ideal job
Past simple tense *be* Past simple tense regular and irregular verbs	Our new apartment A bad trip A lost item A bad dinner date Recent trips	Adjectives for feelings and emotions Everyday activities	**Reading** *Learning Vacation Reviews* **Writing** A vacation review
Be going to and *will*	Weekend plans An invitation for the holidays Who is going to come to the party? A visit to New York City	Things to do over the holidays Expressions for the future	**Reading** *Unusual Tours* **Writing** My holiday plans An invitation notice A three-day trip

Getting Ready

Let's learn some useful classroom sentences.

Your teacher says . . .

Raise your hand.
Open your book.
Write this down.
Find a partner.
Turn to page (number).
Work in groups of (number).

Students say . . .

I don't understand.
Could you repeat that, please?
Speak more slowly, please.
How do you spell (word)?
How do I say (word or phrase) in English?

Unit

1

Introducing Myself

Warm-up

A How do you say hello in English? Check the sentences you know.

Q. Say hello in your country's language.

B How do you greet people in your country? Check the correct picture(s).

My name is Maria Smith.

Conversation

Listen and practice the conversations. 01-01

A Hi. My name is Maria. What's your name?
B My name is Shinichi.

A Hello. My name is Ken. I'm glad to meet you.
B Hi. I am Pedro. I'm glad to meet you, too.

A I'm Ricardo. Nice to meet you.
B My name is Chen. Nice to meet you, too.

A Hey, Clara. What is our new English teacher's name?
B Her name is Sharon.

Names

Look at some popular names in each region.

America	Latin America	Europe	Asia
Michael, Amy, David, Chris, Emily	Maria, Pedro, Juan, Sofia, Isabella	Pierre, Hans, Lola, Mia, Gretchen, Enrico	Hiro, Jinhee, Tao, Haruko, Fatima

Q. What are some popular names in your country?

Pair Work

Ask your partner's name.

A What is your name?
B My name is Chen Wang.

A What's your name?
B I am John Smith.

* What's = What is

Vocabulary | Titles

Mr.	Miss	Mrs.	Ms.
single or married man	single woman	married woman	single or married woman

Q. Look at the names below. Who is single? Who is a man?
Mr. John Smith / Miss Anna Romanov / Mrs. Greta Horst / Ms. Susan Bradley

Grammar | Possessive Adjectives

A Let's learn about possessive adjectives.

I / my	you / your	he / his	she / her	it / its
we / our	you / your		they / their	

* -'s with a singular noun: Sally**'s**
-' with a plural noun: classmates**'**

What is **your** name? - **My** name is Karen.
What are **their** names? - **Their** names are Ren and Souta.
What's the **man's** name? - **His** name is Mark Anderson.

B Choose the correct words.

1. He is a student. (He / His) name is Sam.
2. I am a teacher. (I / My) name is Lisa.
3. They are doctors. (Their / They) names are Brett and Yuka.
4. We are sisters. (We / Our) names are Ahn and Chun.
5. She is a professor. (Her / She) name is Mrs. Jackson.
6. It is a dog. (It's / Its) name is Coffee.
7. They are friends. (Their / Them) names are Claudia and Fritz.

TIPS & TIPS First Names, Middle Names, and Last Names

Scott	Eric	Hampton
↙	↓	↘
first name	middle name	last / family name

Group Work Make a nametag with your full name. Show it to your group members. Then ask other people their names.

A What is the student's name?
B She is Jessie Bernard.

A What is his family name?
B His family name is Zimmer.

A What is our English teacher's name?
B His name is Mr. Jenkins.

I am from Mexico.

Nationalities

Country	Nationality	Country	Nationality
England	English	Japan	Japanese
France	French	China	Chinese
Spain	Spanish	Korea	Korean
Germany	German	Australia	Australian
Switzerland	Swiss	Vietnam	Vietnamese
Italy	Italian	Thailand	Thai
Russia	Russian	Malaysia	Malaysian
United States	American	India	Indian
Canada	Canadian	Saudi Arabia	Saudi Arabian
Mexico	Mexican	Egypt	Egyptian
Argentina	Argentinian	Greece	Greek

Q. List some other countries and nationalities you know.

Conversation

Listen and practice the conversations. 01-02

A Where are you from?
B I'm from Spain. I'm Spanish.

A Are you from Malaysia?
B No, I'm not. I'm from Vietnam. I'm Vietnamese.

A Where is your family from?
B We are from Canada. We're Canadian.

A Hello. Are you Korean?
B No, I'm not. I'm Japanese. I'm from Japan.

Pair Work

Talk about the nationalities of some famous people with your partner.

A Where is Lady GaGa from?
B She is American.

A Where is Cristiano Ronaldo from?
B He is from Portugal.

Listening

A Listen to the people introducing themselves. Then check the correct countries. 01-03

1. ☐ Philippines ☐ China ☐ Vietnam
2. ☐ England ☐ Norway ☐ Germany
3. ☐ Mexico ☐ Argentina ☐ Chile

B Listen to each person talk. Where is each person from?

1. a. Italy b. Greece c. France
2. a. Guyana b. Colombia c. Argentina
3. a. Switzerland b. Australia c. Germany
4. a. India b. Italy c. China
5. a. United States b. United Kingdom c. United Arab Emirates

Group Work

Ask your group members about their nationalities. Then make a list.

A What is your name?
B My name is Tyler.
A Where are you from?
B I am from Italy.

A What is your name?
B I am Ian.
A Where are you from?
B I'm English.

My Classmates' Countries					
Name					
Country					

What's your phone number?

Numbers and Email Addresses

Let's learn numbers and email addresses.

Number

0 zero	1 one	2 two
3 three	4 four	5 five
6 six	7 seven	8 eight
9 nine	10 ten	

Q. Read the numbers.

245-4531-4015
56-487-5144

Email Address

@ at	. dot
_ underscore	- dash

com = company
org = organization
ac = academy
edu = education
net = network

Q. Read the email addresses.

mike@abcz.com
wang_sue@chianir.org
sumilee@personalmail.net
erika_hoff55@gardener.com

Conversation

Listen and practice the conversation. 01-04

A John, what's your telephone number?
B It's 604-5856.
A 604-5865?
B No, it's 604-5856.
A What's your email address?
B It's johnny_st@kto.org.
A Thanks.

Pair Work

Ask your partner his or her phone number and email address.

A Mary, what's your telephone number?
B It's 706-1325.

A Juan, what's your email address?
B It's juan-rodz@yeok.com.

Listening

Listen to the voice messages. Then choose the correct numbers or email addresses. 01-05

1. a. 478-7898 b. 487-7676
2. a. j-maunder@privatemail.com b. j_maunder@privatemail.org
3. a. 925-6291 b. 925-6192
4. a. kate_85@etz.edu b. cathy_85@ecs.edu

Speaking

Look at the four business cards. Then say each phone number and email address.

Tony Lee's phone number is 452-0248-7456. His email address is t_lee@ssl.org.

Group Work

Make your own business cards. Give them to your group members. Then read the other members' phone numbers and email addresses.

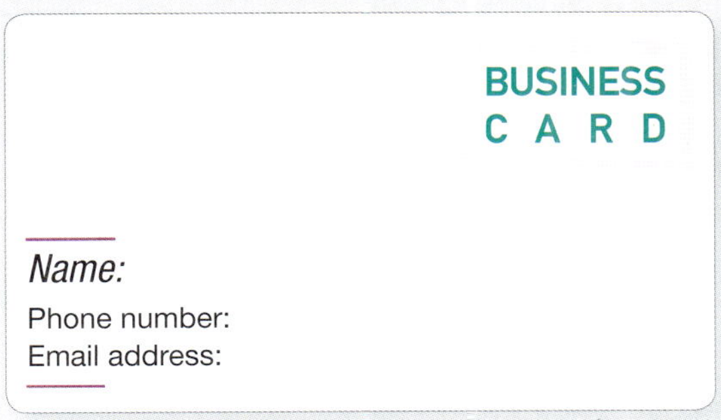

She's a chef.

Reading

Read the articles about various jobs. 01-06

Mario Eco is an artist. He's from Florence, Italy. He's Italian. Mario works in Rome. He paints pictures all day.

Jenny Stewart is from the United States. She's a chef. She works at a restaurant in Chicago. She loves cooking pasta.

Jing Li is Chinese. She's from Shanghai, China. She lives in Beijing. She is a tour guide. She takes visitors to many places.

Pedro Rodriguez is Chilean. He's from Chile. He drives a bus. He drives his bus in Santiago every day.

Comprehension Check Complete the sentences about the articles.

1. Mario Eco works in ______________. He's ______________.
2. Jenny Stewart is ______________. She works in ______________.
3. Jing Li lives in ______________. She's a ______________.
4. ______________ is a bus driver. He's ______________.

Vocabulary | Jobs

A Put the numbers in the correct places.

☐ doctor

☐ police officer

☐ pilot

☐ actor/actress

☐ singer

☐ soccer player

1. makes people safe
2. flies airplanes
3. helps sick people
4. plays soccer
5. sings songs
6. performs on TV or in movies

B What are some popular jobs in your country? Talk about them with your partner.

A Doctor is a popular job in my country.
B What does a doctor do?
A A doctor helps sick people.

Group Work

A Tell your group members about a famous person. Your group members guess who it is.

A He is a famous soccer player. He's from Argentina. Who is he?
B Is he Messi?
A Yes, you're right.

B List some famous people you know. What are their full names? What are their jobs and nationalities? Tell your classmates about them. Then complete the table.

A Do you know Johnny Depp?
B No. Who is he?
A He's a famous movie star. He is American.

	First Name	Last Name	Job	Nationality
	Johnny	*Depp*	*Actor*	*American*
1.				
2.				
3.				
4.				

Writing

Think about your favorite celebrity. What is that person's job? Write a short essay about that person.

My Favorite Celebrity
My favorite person is Tom Cruise. He is American. He is an actor and movie star. I love the Mission Impossible *movies.*

Wrap-up

A Answer the questions with your own information.

1. What is the next person's name?
2. What is your English teacher's family name?
3. What is your father's full name? Where is he from?

B Complete the table with the correct words.

Country	Nationality	Country	Nationality
France			Chinese
	German	Australia	
Italy			Vietnamese
United States		Malaysia	
Mexico		Saudi Arabia	

C Say three countries you want to visit in the future.

D Write your best friend's phone number and email address. Then read them.

My best friend's phone number is ______________________________.

His/Her email address is ______________________________.

E Describe a job. Your partner guesses it.

A I help people.
B Are you a police officer?
A No. I help sick people.
B Are you a doctor?
A Yes, I am.

F Go online and search for the most famous sports star and movie star in your country. Then write about the two people.

Unit 2

My Family and Friends

Warm-up

A Look at the picture and complete the sentences with the correct words.

grandparents & grandchildren

parents & children

Greg Dawson (husband) - Julie Dawson (wife)

Tim Dawson (brother) - Amy Dawson (sister)

* **uncle**: father's or mother's brother   **aunt**: father's or mother's sister

1. Lisa Dawson is Amy Dawson's ______________.
2. Tim Dawson is Julie Dawson's ______________.
3. Greg Dawson and Julie Dawson are Tim Dawson's ______________.
4. Julie Dawson is Greg Dawson's ______________.

B Make your own family tree.

Do you have a sister?

Conversation

Listen and practice the conversation. 02-01

A Do you have a sister?
B Yes. My sister's name is Jessica.
A How old is your sister?
B She is 21 years old.
A Is she a student?
B No, she works at a library.

Vocabulary | Numbers

11	12	13	14	15	16	17	18	19
eleven	twelve	thirteen	fourteen	fifteen	sixteen	seventeen	eighteen	nineteen
20	30	40	50	60	70	80	90	100
twenty	thirty	forty	fifty	sixty	seventy	eighty	ninety	one hundred

Pair Work

Ask your partner about his or her family members.

A Do you have a brother?
B Yes, I do.
A How old is he?
B He is 13.

A Do you have a sister?
B Yes. Her name is Michelle.
A Is she a student?
B No, she is a housewife.

TIPS & TIPS More Numbers

21	32	43	101	1,000	1,000,000
twenty-one	thirty-two	forty-three	one hundred one	one thousand	one million

Grammar

A Let's ask questions with *do ~ have* and *how old*.

Do you **have** a brother?	- No, I **don't**. I only **have** one sister.
Do you **have** an aunt?	- Yes, I **do**. I **have** three aunts.
Does he **have** a son?	- Yes, he **does**. He **has** two sons.
How old is he?	- He is **12**.
How old is she?	- She is **44** years old.
How old are they?	- They're **5**, **6**, and **8**.

* They're = They are

B Complete the conversations with the correct questions.

1. A ________________________________?
   B Yes, I do. I have one sister.
2. A ________________________________?
   B He is 59 years old.
3. A ________________________________?
   B Yes, she does. She has three daughters.
4. A ________________________________?
   B They are 20, 22, and 25.

Group Work Make a table with your family member's names, ages, and jobs. Then talk about your family with your group members.

	Name	Age	Job
	Sarah Jones	*52*	*computer programmer*
1.			
2.			
3.			

I have a mother. Her name is Sarah Jones.
She is 52 years old. She is a computer programmer.

They are both kind!

Personalities and Appearances

A Let's learn some adjectives for personalities and appearances.

Personalities	quiet, shy, funny, lazy, calm, kind / good / nice / friendly, outgoing, smart, talkative
Appearances	tall, short, thin, young, old, cute / adorable, pretty / beautiful, fat / overweight / heavy

B Describe the woman in the picture.

I think she is ....

....

....

Q. Talk about your own personality and appearance.

Reading

Read a short article about Karen's family. Then complete the table. 02-02

Hello, everyone. My name is Karen. I live with my grandparents. My grandfather's name is John Lewis. He is 72 years old. He is from Australia. My grandmother is Catherine Lewis. She is 65 years old. She is from England. My grandfather is tall. But my grandmother is short. They are both kind!

	Name	Age	Nationality	Appearance	Personality
Karen's grandfather					
Karen's grandmother					

Listening

A Listen to the talk. Then write each family member's name in the picture. 02-03

Kevin	Jonathan	Nancy	Catherine

B Listen again and check the words you hear.

☐ nice ☐ cute ☐ thick ☐ tall ☐ smart ☐ calm ☐ outgoing

C Listen again and choose the correct answers.

1. Nancy is ______________.
   a. Jonathan's wife b. Catherine's sister c. Jonathan's daughter
2. Catherine is ______________.
   a. nice b. smart c. outgoing
3. ______________ loves soccer.
   a. Jonathan b. Nancy c. Kevin

Group Work Make a list with your family member's personalities and appearances. Then talk about them with your group members.

A My father is kind and fat. My mother is talkative and tall.
B How old is your father?

Who is this?

Conversation

Listen and practice the conversation. 02-04

A Who is this?
B He is my best friend. His name is Wang. He's from China.
A How old is he?
B He is twenty-two.
A Is he a student?
B No, he isn't. He works at a hotel.
A Who are they?
B They are my friends. The woman is Julie.
The man is Juan.
A Are they students?
B Yes. We are classmates.

Vocabulary | More Jobs

accountant

architect

baker

butcher

carpenter

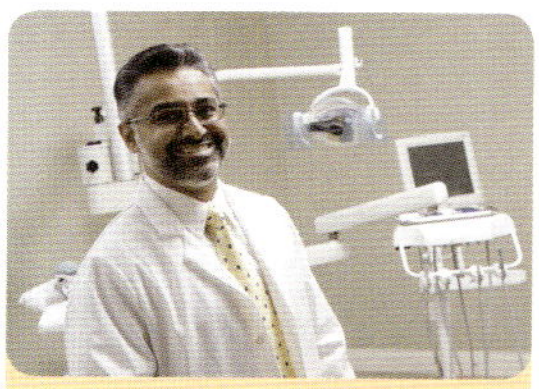
dentist

farmer

mechanic

nurse

teacher

Q. Say some other jobs you know.

Pair Work

Show a picture of your friend to your partner. Then talk about him or her.

A He is my friend, Akira. He is a student.
B Where is he from?
A He is Japanese.

A She is Angela. She works at a restaurant.
B Is she kind?
A Yes, she is. And she is very funny.

Listening

A Listen to the people talk about their friends. Then choose the correct answers. 02-05

1. Sarah is a ______________.
   a. student　　b. teacher　　c. firefighter
2. John is ______________.
   a. 19　　b. 29　　c. 39
3. He is from ______________.
   a. China　　b. South Korea　　c. Japan

B Listen to Tim talk about his friends. Then match the pictures to the correct names.

1. 

2. 

3. 

4. 

David　　Tommy　　Karen　　Kevin

C Listen again and answer the questions.

1. Who is Kevin?
2. How old is Karen?
3. Where is David from?
4. Is Tommy a student?
5. Who works at a restaurant?

Writing

Describe some of your friends.

My Friends

Sam is my friend. He is 21 years old. He is from England. He is a student. Jane is my friend, too . . .

People I Know

Reading

Read the articles about these four people. 02-06

Ryan is my classmate. He is in a blue T-shirt in the picture. He is 19 years old. He is smart and a good student. He is from England.

Julie is my English teacher. She is from Sydney, Australia. Her last name is Lee. She likes blouses and skirts. She is really nice to every student.

This is Ricardo, a friend from high school. He always wears a cap and glasses. He loves music. He is a good singer and guitarist. He is very tall.

Cathy is my neighbor. She is 33 years old. She has long black hair. She is friendly and outgoing. She is a good cook. I like her food.

Comprehension Check Answer the questions about the articles.

1. Who is smart?
2. Is Ricardo short?
3. Where is Julie from?
4. Does Julie like blue jeans?
5. How old is Cathy?

Vocabulary | Colors, Clothes, and Accessories

A Complete the table with the correct words.

1.	blue	2.	3.	brown	4.	purple	5.	6.	white

B Match the words and phrases to the correct pictures.

T-shirt | blue jeans | blouse | skirt | shorts | glasses | cap | necklace | earrings

1. 
____

2. 
____

3. 
____

4. 
____

5. 
____

6. 
____

7. 
____

8. 
____

9. 
____

Class Activity

A Describe yourself to the class.

I am short. I have short black hair. I always wear a T-shirt and blue jeans. I like caps, too.

B Think of a student in your class. Your classmates guess who he or she is.

A Is it a man?
B No, it isn't.
A Is she quiet?
B Yes, she is.
A Does she wear glasses?

Presentation

Draw your best friend. Then describe his or her clothes and accessories.

Wrap-up

A Answer the questions with your own information.

1. Do you have a brother or sister?
2. Does your father have a brother or sister?
3. How old is your mother?

B Put the words in the correct places.

outgoing tall thin kind shy talkative pretty young

Appearances	Personalities

C Ask your partner questions about his or her best friend.

A What is your best friend's name?
B Her name is Donna.
A How old is she?
B She is 23 years old.
A Is she a student?
B No, she is an English teacher.

D Describe the people's appearances. Then guess their personalities.

1.

2.

3.

Unit 3

Things

Warm-up

A Look at the pictures and choose the correct words.

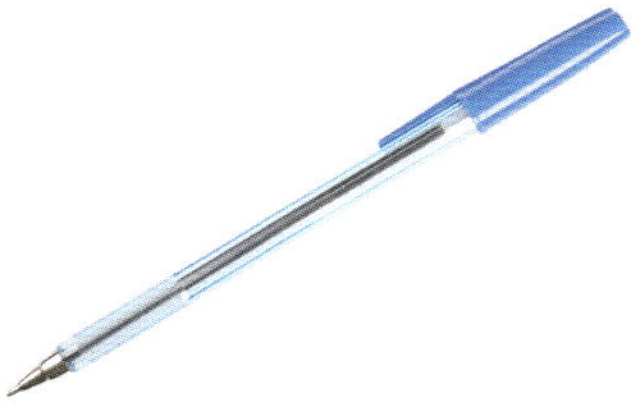

1. pencil / pen

2. note / computer

3. chair / desk

4. bag / hat

5. wallet / belt

6. lock / key

B What's in your bag? Check the items you have in your bag.

- ☐ camera
- ☐ charger
- ☐ headphones
- ☐ laptop / tablet
- ☐ mobile phone
- ☐ notebooks
- ☐ pencils / pens
- ☐ wallet

Q. What else do you have in your bag?

What's in your bag?

Conversation

Listen and practice the conversation. 03-01

A Petra, what do you have in your bag?
B Well, I have books, lipstick, a wallet, and hand lotion. How about you?
A There are books, a laptop, pens, and pencils.
B Wow. Do you need help with your bag?
A No, thanks. It's not that heavy.

Vocabulary | Items

Look at the picture. Then find the things in it.

- ☐ laptop
- ☐ watch
- ☐ USB drive
- ☐ ruler
- ☐ notebooks
- ☐ glasses

Listening

A Listen to the conversation and check the correct answers. 03-02

1. What is on Pierre's desk?
   a. a watch b. a pencil c. a notebook
2. Where are Pierre's glasses?
   a. on his desk b. on his face c. on his bed

B Listen again and choose True or False.

1. Pierre has a dirty desk. [True / False]
2. Pierre does not have a USB drive. [True / False]

Grammar | Nouns

A Let's learn about singular and plural nouns.

I have **a bag**. I have **two bags**.	Linda needs **a pen**. Linda needs **three pens**.	There is **a notebook** on the desk. There are **many notebooks** on the desk.

* **an** + a vowel sound: **an e**ye, **an e**ar, **an e**raser, **an i**ce cream cone
Noun ending in s, x, z, ch, sh + -**es**: wat**ches**, bus**es**, fox**es**, wish**es**

B Choose the correct words.

1. I have (a / an) apple.
2. We are (a brother / brothers).
3. The farmer has twenty (horsees / horses).
4. He can move the heavy (boxs / boxes).
5. I want to see (a /an) doctor.
6. I want a house with (a / an) yard.
7. Two (boys / boyes) are playing soccer.
8. The zoo has three (a bear / bears).
9. Allan and Laura are (a student / students).
10. He has one (car / cars).

Pair Work

Borrow something from your partner.

A Do you have an eraser?
B Yes, I do.
A Can I borrow it?
B Sure. Here it is.

A Do you have chopsticks?
B Yes, I do.
A Can I borrow them?
B Sure. Here they are.

What is this?

Conversation

Listen and practice the conversation. 03-03

A Wow, I really like your kitchen.
B Thanks.
A What's this?
B This is my coffee maker.
A Cool. What are those over there?
B Those are my new cookbooks. I like cooking.
A And these?
B These are oven mitts from my grandmother.
A They're so cute! By the way, where is the bathroom?
B Oh, it's through that door.

Grammar | Demonstrative Pronouns

Let's learn about the demonstrative pronouns *this*, *that*, *these*, and *those*.

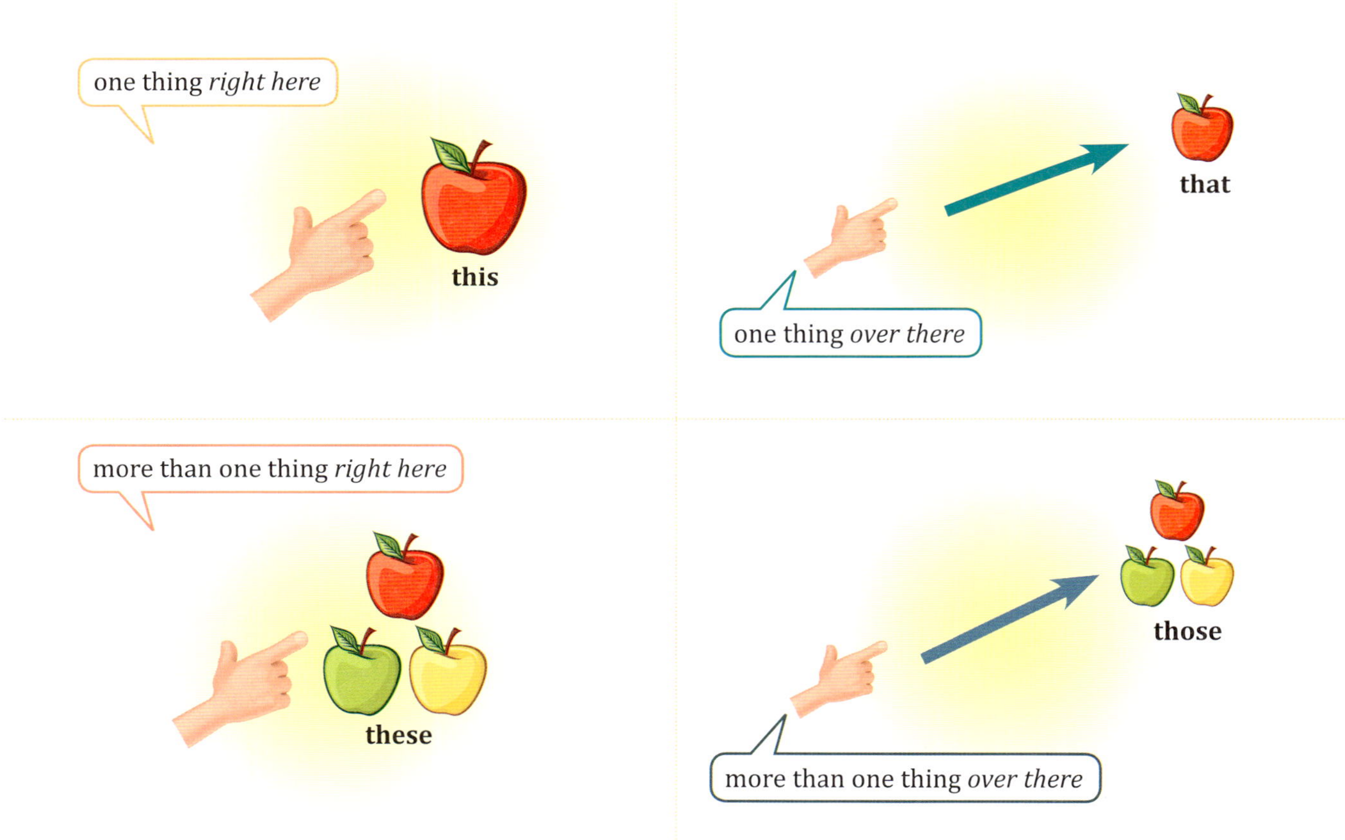

TIPS & TIPS Possessive Adjectives and Nouns

This is a bag. (o)
This is a one bag. (x)

This is my bag. (o)
This is a my bag. (x)

These are my bags. (o)
These are a bags. (x)

Pair Work

A Look around. Then write two things for each category. What items are on your partner's list?

this	that	these	those
pencil			

B Practice the conversations with your partner.

A What is this?
B This is my bag.

A What are these?
B These are my books.

A What is that?
B That is a window.

A What are those?
B Those are posters.

Listening

A Listen and complete the conversation. 03-04

A How do you like the room?
B It's very nice. I like it.
A ______________ is my bed, so ______________ is yours.
B Cool.
A You can use ______________ bookshelves over ______________.
Oh, here. ______________ are the keys to the ______________.
B Thanks.

B Listen again and answer the questions.

1. Who are the speakers?
   a. a teacher and a student
   b. two roommates
   c. a sister and a brother

2. What is in the room?
   a. a bed and bookshelves
   b. two beds
   c. two beds and bookshelves

3. What are the keys for?
   a. the house
   b. the room
   c. the bookshelf

Which one is it?

Conversation

Listen and practice the conversation. 03-05

A I want my gift!
B It's under the tree in front of the TV.
A Great. Which one is it?
B It's a red box.
A There are two red boxes. Is it by the yellow one?
B No. That's for Mom. It's behind the white box.
It has a green ribbon on the top.
A Aha. I see it. Thanks.

Grammar | Prepositions of Place 1

Let's learn some prepositions.

in

on

under

by

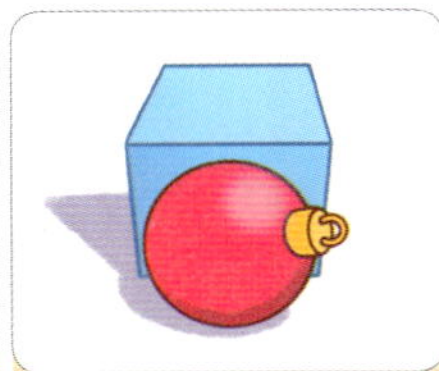

in front of

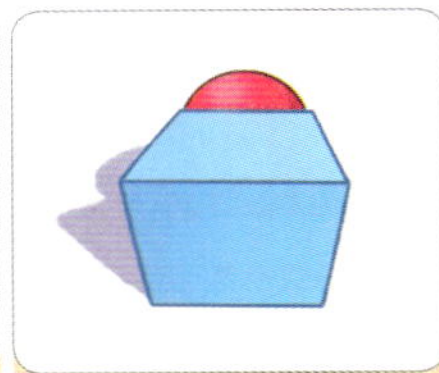

behind

Speaking

A Look at the pictures. Then say where the things are.

1.

The car is in front of the building.

2.

3.

4.

5.

6.

B Answer the questions with your own information.

1. What's on your desk?

2. Who is in front of you? Say his or her name.

Listening

A Listen and complete the conversation. 03-06

A I really like that purple bag ____________ the top shelf.

B It's not ____________. But I like the green one ____________ the hats better.

A Hmm . . . I don't know. I don't like ____________.

B How about the dark blue bag ____________ the table?

A The small one? It's actually ____________. I like it.

B Do you want to go in and ask the ____________?

A Sure. Wait. Where is my little sister?

B Turn around. She is right ____________ you.

B Listen again and choose the correct answers.

1. Where are the speakers?

   a. at home　　b. in a store　　c. in front of a store

2. Which bag do the speakers want to ask the price of?

   a. the purple bag　　b. the green bag　　c. the dark blue bag

Pair Work

A Look at the picture. Then find the items in the box with your partner.

blue ball	clocks	yellow	ball
computers	lamp	bin	shelf

A Where is the blue ball?
B It's behind the blue box.

A Where are the clocks?
B They are on the wall.

B Draw your room. Then describe it to your partner.

I have . . . in my room. The bed is . . . My desk and chair are . . .

I am messy.

Rate Yourself

A Are you tidy or messy? Why do you think so?

B Look at the pictures and choose the words that best match you.

My bedroom is . . .

My desk is . . .

My closet is . . .

Pair Work

Ask your partner some questions about his or her room and roommate.

A Do you have your own room?
B No, I share a room with my brother.

A Is your room dirty?
B No, it's not. My roommate Nancy always cleans the room.

Reading

Read about James. 03-07

My name is James. I am messy. Alex is my roommate. He is clean. He wants me to clean the room with him. But I am too busy. I study every day. I have a lot of homework, too. When I finish my homework, I am too tired. I just want to sleep. I put my clothes on my bed. I put my books on my desk. Alex still gets angry with me. I don't know why. But I want to be clean in the future.

Comprehension Check Answer the questions about the article.

1. Who is messy?
2. Who is clean?
3. Why does Alex get angry with James?
4. How many desks are there? How many beds are there?
5. What does James want to be in the future?

Writing

Do you know anybody like James in the article? Who is that person? How messy is he or she? Write a short essay about that person.

Kate is messy. She is my younger sister. She is 14 years old. She is lazy . . .

Group Work Read your essay to your group. Then listen to other members' essays and complete the table.

	Classmate's Name	Who is messy?	Relationship
	Sandy	*Bill*	*her brother*
1.			
2.			
3.			

Wrap-up

A What's in your bag? Complete the sentence.

I have ___*a wallet*___, ______________, and ______________ in my bag.

B Complete the table with the correct words.

one (singular)	**more than one** (plural)
an apple	
	shoes
a bus	
	erasers

C Look at the pictures and complete the sentences with *this*, *that*, *these*, or *those*.

1. 

___________ is a bench.

2. 

___________ is a bench.

3. 

___________ are students.

4. 

___________ are students.

D Look at the picture and answer the questions.

1. Where is the bicycle?
   → It is ______________ the wall.
2. Where is the desk?
   → It is ______________ the window.
3. Where are the magazines?
   → They are ______________ the table.

Unit 4

Daily Life

Warm-up

A Look at the picture and put the words in the correct places.

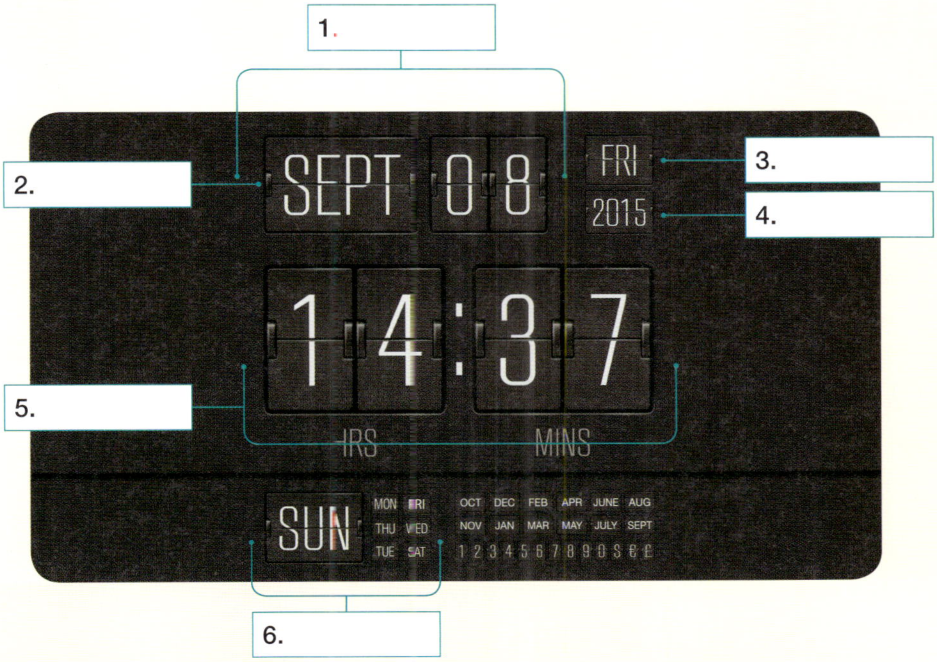

time
day
week
month
year
date

B What activities do the people in the pictures do? When do they do these things? How about you?

1.

2.

3.

4.

5.

6.

My show is on.

Conversation

Listen and practice the conversation. 04-01

A What day is it today?
B It's Wednesday. Why?
A My favorite TV show is on.
B What is it?
A It's called *Three Sisters*. Do you want to watch it?
B Sure. When does it start?
A At eight o'clock.

TIPS & TIPS Title

* It's *Three Sisters*. = Its title is *Three Sisters*. = It's called *Three Sisters*.

Pair Work

Ask your partner about his or her favorite TV show.

A What is your favorite TV show?
B It is *Wild Animals*.
A When is it on?
B It is on Saturday at 3 p.m.

TV Schedule

Look at the TV schedule. Then answer the questions below.

Wednesday Evening TV Schedule					
Time	Channel 04	Channel 05	Channel 09	Channel 11	Channel 29
8:00 p.m. - 9:00 p.m.	The Cooking Show Love in the Country	Real History	Three Sisters	Education Hour Comedy Time	Baseball
9:00 p.m. -10:00 p.m.	CBH News Show	Wonderful Nature	Super Girl	The World News	Today's Movie

1. When does the television program *The Cooking Show* start?
2. What channel is *Real History* on?
3. What time does *The World News* start?
4. What is on Channel 09 at eight o'clock?
5. When does the baseball game end?

Vocabulary | Telling Time

A Let's learn how to tell time.

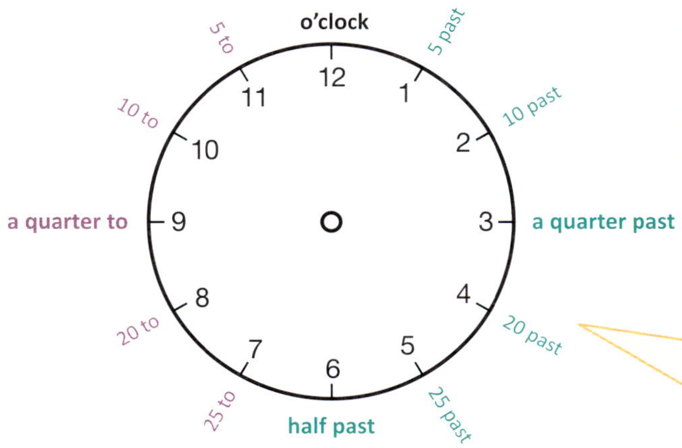

What time is it?

7:00	*It's seven **o'clock**.*
1:05	*It's **five past** one.*
7:30	*It's **half past** seven.*
4:45	*It's **a quarter to** five.*
5:15	*It's **a quarter past** five.*
2:10	*It's **ten past** two.*
11:5	*It's **ten to** twelve.*
9:55	*It's **five to** ten.*
12:00	*It's twelve **o'clock**. / It's **noon**. / It's **midnight**.*

B Write the correct times.

1. 

   ____

2. 

   ____

3. 

   ten to six

4. 

   half past four

Listening

Listen to the conversations. Then write the times you hear. 04-02

1. ______ : ______
2. ______ : ______
3. ______ : ______
4. ______ : ______

Pair Work

Practice the conversations with your partner.

A What time is it?
B It's ____________.

A When is your next break?
B It is at ____________.

A When does this class finish?
B It finishes at ____________.

A When do you wake up?
B ____________.

I get up at 7 o'clock.

Grammar | Present Simple Tense

A Let's learn about the present simple tense.

I **get up** at 7 o'clock. Hank **gets up** at 6 o'clock. You **walk** to work. The students **come** to school at 8:30 a.m.	I **don't** eat breakfast every day. She **doesn't go** to school on weekends. **Does** the bus **come** every hour? - Yes, it **does**. / No, it **doesn't**. Do you **watch** TV after 11 p.m.? - Yes, I **do**. / No, I **don't**.

* don't = do not doesn't = does not

B Complete the sentences with the correct forms of the verbs.

1. I ______________ breakfast at 6:30 in the morning. (eat)
2. Pam ______________ her house before 7:45 a.m. (not / leave)
3. I ______________ the bus to work in the morning. (take)
4. He ______________ lunch at 12:30 p.m. (have)
5. The workers ______________ home at 6:00 p.m. (go)
6. We ______________ TV in the evening. (not / watch)
7. ______________ you ______________ to bed at 11:00 p.m? (go)

Pair Work Talk about Michiko's typical Monday schedule with your partner.

A Does Michiko do yoga on Monday morning?
B No, she doesn't.
A What does Michiko do on Monday morning then?
B She plays tennis.

Michiko's Monday	
10 ~ 11 a.m.	play tennis
1 p.m.	have lunch
2 p.m.	go to work
11:30 p.m.	go to bed

Writing

A What are your typical Mondays like? Write about them.

On Monday mornings, I ....

On Monday afternoons, I ....

On Monday evenings, I ....

B How about your Sundays? Write about them.

....

Reading

Read about Janice's and Sam's typical days. 04-03

Hi. I'm Janice. I'm a student. In the mornings, I go to school. On Monday and Wednesday afternoons, I go to the gym. On Tuesday and Thursday afternoons, I do my homework. On Friday afternoons, I meet my friends at a coffee shop. In the evenings, I watch TV. I don't go to bed before 11 p.m.

Hi. My name is Sam. I'm a bartender. I wake up and drink coffee in the mornings. On Monday afternoons, I go grocery shopping. On Tuesday and Thursday afternoons, I study Chinese. On Wednesday and Friday afternoons, I go for a walk. In the evenings, I work at a bar. I finish work late at night, so I go to sleep after 2 a.m.

Comprehension Check **Answer the questions about Janice's and Sam's schedules.**

1. Does Janice go to the gym on Mondays and Wednesdays?
2. Who goes grocery shopping on Monday afternoons?
3. What does Sam do on Tuesday and Thursday afternoons?
4. Complete the table about Janice's and Sam's Friday schedules.

Friday	Janice	Sam
Morning	She ______________.	He drinks coffee.
Afternoon	She meets her friends at a coffee shop.	He ______________.
Evening	She ______________.	He ______________.

TIPS & TIPS The Days of the Week

Monday	Tuesday	Wednesday	Thursday	Friday	Saturday	Sunday

weekdays (Monday – Friday)

the weekend (Saturday – Sunday)

How's your sister?

Conversation

Listen and practice the conversation. 04-04

A Hey, Janelle! How is your sister?
B She's great. She plans to study in England.
A When does she leave?
B On June 2nd. Her plane leaves at 5 a.m.
A That's very early.
B I know. She has to wake up at 2 a.m.

Vocabulary | Ordinal Numbers

A Let's learn about ordinal numbers.

1st	first	9th	ninth	24th	twenty-fourth
2nd	second	10th	tenth	30th	thirtieth
3rd	third	11th	eleventh	31st	thirty-first
4th	fourth	12th	twelfth	50th	fiftieth
5th	fifth	20th	twentieth	80th	eightieth
6th	sixth	21st	twenty-first	100th	one hundredth
7th	seventh	22nd	twenty-second	1,000th	one thousandth
8th	eighth	23rd	twenty-third	1,000,000th	one millionth

* the + ordinal numbers

The wedding is on the 1st of February. (o)
The wedding is on 1st of February. (x)

Sam's office is on the 2nd floor. (o)
Sam's office is on 2nd floor. (x)

B Read the sentences.

1. The office is on the 1st floor.
2. Alex lives on the 3rd floor.
3. They leave on the 10th of April.
4. His birthday is on the 12th.

C Look at the picture. Then write the correct ordinal numbers.

Grammar | *In, On, and At*

A Let's learn about the prepositions *in*, *on*, and *at*.

in + months/year	**in** January	**in** 1997	
on + days/the weekend/dates	**on** Wednesday	**on** the weekend	**on** May 26th
at + time	**at** seven o'clock	**at** 8:30	

Halloween is **in** October. His birthday is **on** March 22nd. He usually calls **at** 7:00.

B Complete the sentences with *in*, *on*, or *at*.

1. She plans to go to Europe _____ 2017.
2. Tom lives _____ China.
3. Christmas is _____ December 25th.
4. Mary finishes work _____ 6:00 p.m.
5. We celebrate Thanksgiving _____ November.
6. She usually goes shopping _____ Saturday.

Listening

A Listen and complete the conversation. 04-05

A John, do you want to come to my _______________ party?
B Sure. _______________ is it, Mika?
A It's _______________ March 2nd _______________ o'clock.
B Where is it?
A It's at Tony's Pizzeria.
B That _______________ great!

B Listen again and choose True or False.

1. The speakers are talking about John's birthday party. [True / False]
2. The party starts at six o'clock. [True / False]

Pair Work Choose a role card. Then invite your partner to your party.

	Student A	Student B
Party Type Date Time / Place	graduation party October 12th 8:30 p.m. / Jane's house	Christmas party December 19th 6:45 p.m. / Peter's office

TIPS & TIPS Months and Their Abbreviations

January = Jan.	February = Feb.	March = Mar.	April = Apr.
May = May	June = Jun.	July = Jul.	August = Aug.
September = Sept.	October = Oct.	November = Nov.	December = Dec.

I never take the bus.

Reading

Read the story about Margaret. 04-06

Hi. My name is Margaret. I'm an office worker. I always wake up at 6 a.m. I usually exercise and drink coffee in the morning. I always drive to work. I never take the bus. Sometimes I buy bread at the bakery near my office. I usually eat the bread at my desk. I always have lunch in the company cafeteria. I usually finish work at six o'clock. In the evenings, I read books. I rarely watch TV. I go to bed at 10 p.m.

Comprehension Check Answer the questions with *always*, *usually*, *sometimes*, *rarely*, or *never*.

1. How often does Margaret wake up at 6 a.m.?
2. How often does Margaret take the bus to work?
3. How often does Margaret buy bread in the mornings?
4. How often does Margaret watch TV in the evenings?

Vocabulary | Adverbs of Frequency

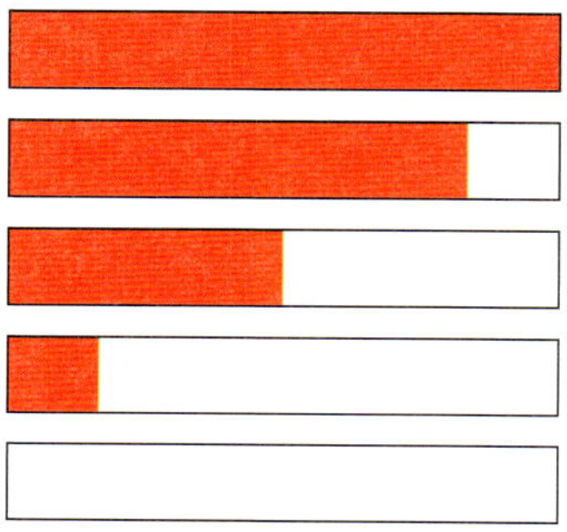

	How often do you do . . . ?
Always	I **always** drink coffee after lunch.
Usually	She **usually** exercises in the morning.
Sometimes	Jonathan **sometimes** eats lunch with his girlfriend.
Rarely	They **rarely** visit their hometowns.
Never	My husband and I **never** wake up late.

Class Activity

Ask three classmates the questions with *How often do you ~?* Write *always*, *usually*, *sometimes*, *rarely*, or *never* in the table. Then tell the class about your survey results.

How often do you . . . ?	Name:	Name:	Name:
go to the movies			
wash your car			
go dancing			
drink alcohol			
do the dishes			

Wrap-up

A Look at the pictures and read the times.

1. 

nine ______________

2. 

twelve ______________

3. 

________ after ________

4. 

________ past ________

B Complete the sentences with the correct forms of the verbs.

1. I ____________ at 8:30 a.m. (get up)
2. She ____________ a taxi to work in the morning. (take)
3. He ____________ to bed at 12:00 a.m. (not / go)

C Complete the sentences with true information. Then read them.

1. Today is ______________.
   (date)
2. Today is ______________.
   (day)

D Look at the table. Then answer the questions with *always*, *usually*, *sometimes*, *rarely*, or *never*.

Jill's Activities during the Week							
activity	Mon	Tues	Wed	Thu	Fri	Sat	Sun
get up late						O	
do the dishes	O	O	O	O	O	O	O
drive to work		O		O		O	
exercise							

1. How often does Jill get up late?
2. How often does Jill do the dishes?
3. How often does Jill drive to work?
4. How often does Jill exercise?

Unit
5
Pastimes and Weekends

Warm-up

A Look at Mike's garage. What kinds of sports and activities does he do? Check the names on the list.

□ golf	□ basketball	□ fishing
□ baseball	□ tennis	□ soccer
□ yoga	□ skiing	□ American football

B What sports and activities do you like?

What do you do on the weekend?

Conversation

Listen and practice the conversation. 05-01

A Harry, what do you do on the weekend?
B Well, I play baseball for the company team. How about you?
A I really like to play tennis.
B Really? Do you play with people from our company?
A No, I usually play with my friends. We are in the same tennis club.

Grammar

A Let's learn some expressions about sports and activities.

play + sport	go + -ing	do + sport / activity
play baseball play basketball play tennis play golf	go jogging go swimming go skiing go fishing	do yoga do aerobics do weight training do karate

He **plays baseball** on the weekend.
We **go jogging** on the weekend.
I **do yoga** in the morning.

TIPS & TIPS

I **exercise** every day. = I **work out** every day.
I **go for a walk**. = I take **a walk**.

B Complete the sentences with the correct words.

1. He ____________ baseball on Saturday.
2. I ____________ yoga in the morning.
3. They don't ____________ jogging on Sunday.
4. We ____________ skiing in the winter.
5. John ____________ tennis on the weekend.
6. She ____________ aerobics every day.

Listening

A Listen to the conversation and answer the questions. 05-02

1. What does Caroline do on her day off? Choose the correct picture.

2. What does Ted do on his day off? Choose the correct picture.

a.

b.

c.

d.

B Listen again and choose True or False.

1. Caroline goes jogging with her husband. [True / False]

2. Caroline goes swimming at the park. [True / False]

3. Ted takes his dog for a walk at the school. [True / False]

Pair Work

Look at Ming's schedule. Then ask your partner questions about his weekend schedule.

Ming's Weekend Schedule			
Saturday		Sunday	
9:00 a.m.	play basketball at the park	11:00 a.m.	go hiking with the boss
12:00 p.m.	have lunch with Eric	3:00 p.m.	take a nap
3:00 p.m.	do weight training	6:00 p.m.	go for a walk

A What does Ming do on Saturday at 9:00 a.m.?

B He plays basketball at the park.

Class Activity

Find classmates who do the activities in the table. The first person to get three in a row is the winner.

A Do you play baseball?
B Yes, I do.
A What's your name?
B My name's John.

Tennis	Jogging	Baseball
Name	Name	Name
Basketball	Yoga	Aerobics
Name	Name	Name
Swimming	Soccer	Volleyball
Name	Name	Name

What do you do for fun?

Conversation

Listen and practice the conversation. 05-03

A What do you do for fun?
B I play *Monster Attack*. It's a video game.
A Where do you play it?
B I play it at school.
A Who do you play it with?
B My friends.
A When do you play it?
B During my lunch break.
A Is it fun?
B Yeah! That's why I play it.
A Let me play, too!
B Fine, here!

Grammar | *Who, When,* and *Where*

A Let's learn about *who*, *when*, and *where*.

who	→ person	**Who** is he? **Who** do you play with?	- He is **my friend**. - I play with **my sister**.
when	→ time	**When** do you play basketball?	- I play basketball on **Saturday**.
where	→ place	**Where** do you play basketball?	- We play at **the park**.

B Complete the sentences with *who*, *when*, or *where*.

1. ____________ do you play hockey? - I play it in the winter.
2. ____________ do you play soccer? - We play it on Saturday.
3. ____________ do you play video games with? - I play them with my friends.
4. ____________ do you go swimming? - I go swimming at the city pool.
5. ____________ do you go jogging with? - I go jogging alone.

Speaking

Answer the questions with your own information.

1. What do you do for fun?
2. Who do you do it with?
3. Where do you do it?
4. When do you do it?

Listening

Listen to the conversations and answer the questions. 05-04

1. When does Chen go swimming?
   a. at 9 a.m. on Saturday
   b. at 3 p.m. on Saturday
   c. at 8 a.m. on Thursday

2. Where does Yui play board games?
   a. at her school
   b. at her house
   c. at her grandparents' house

3. Who does Matt go fishing with?
   a. by himself
   b. with his friends
   c. with his dad

Group Work Ask two group members the questions in the table. Then write about the activities they do for fun.

	Name:	Name:
What do you for fun?		
Who do you do it with?		
Where do you do it?		
When do you do it?		

Mike likes to play video games for fun . . .

What do you do on the weekend when it's sunny?

Conversation

Listen and practice the conversation. 05-05

A When is your day off, Kumiko?
B It's every Saturday.
A What do you do when it's sunny on Saturday?
B I go hiking with my sister.
There's a nice mountain near my house.
A What do you do when it's rainy then?
B I read comic books or watch TV.

Vocabulary | Weather and Seasons

Look at the pictures and write the correct words.

Weather

sunny

1. ____________

2. ____________

3. ____________

4. ____________

Seasons

5. ____________

6. ____________

fall

7. ____________

TIPS & TIPS Special Days in the U.S.

Spring	Summer	Fall	Winter
Easter	Independence Day	Halloween	Christmas

People in the U.S. paint eggs on Easter.
Americans watch fireworks on Independence Day.
Many children in the U.S. go trick-or-treating on Halloween.
Americans open presents on Christmas.

Q. What do people in your country do in each season?
Do you have any special days? Say what activities people in your country do on those days.

Grammar | *When*

A Let's learn about *when*.

When do you . . . ? (interrogative)	**When** it's sunny, I ______________. (conjunction)
When is your day off? - My day off is Wednesday. **When** do you go hiking? - I go hiking on the weekend.	I read comic books at home **when** it's rainy. = **When** it's rainy, I read comic books at home. **When** it's stormy, I watch horror movies. I go to the gym **when** I get home from work.

B Complete the sentences.

1. ______________________________? (do aerobics) - I do them every Thursday.
2. Jimmy watches TV ______________________________. (rainy)
3. ______________________________, I play tennis. (have a day off)
4. ______________________________? (go for a walk) - I try to do that every day.

C Complete the sentences with your own information.

1. What do you do for fun? When do you do it?
   → I _________________________. I _________________________.
2. What do you do when it is sunny?
   → When it is sunny, _________________________.

Listening

Listen to the conversation and choose the correct words. 05-06

1. What season does Alex hate? Why?
   → He hates the (winter / summer) because it is too (cold / hot).
2. What does Alex think of the spring?
   → He (doesn't like / likes) the spring because it is rainy.

Pair Work

Ask your partner about his or her favorite season.

A What's your favorite season?
B My favorite season is the spring.
A What sports or activities do you do in the spring?
B I go hiking with my friends.

My Day Off

Reading

A Read Robin's story. 05-07

Hello. I'm Robin. I am a businessman. Many people take a rest on Saturdays. But Saturdays are one of the busiest days of the week for me. On Saturdays, I wake up at 7:00 a.m. In the summer, I play golf with my boss. In the winter, we play tennis at the club. At noon, we have lunch together at a nice restaurant. After lunch, I go shopping at the supermarket and buy food for dinner. I usually get home at 4:00 p.m. In the evening, I cook dinner for my family. We eat dinner at 6 o'clock. After dinner, we play board games. My children go to sleep at 10:00 p.m. When my children go to sleep, my wife and I watch TV. We usually go to sleep at 12:00 a.m.

Comprehension Check Answer the questions about the story.

1. What is Robin's job?
2. Who does Robin play golf with?
3. Where does Robin go in the winter?
4. When does Robin go to the supermarket?
5. What does Robin do in the evening?
6. When do Robin's children go to bed?
7. When does Robin go to sleep?

B Describe Robin's typical Saturday. Use the pictures and phrases.

at 7:00 a.m.

in the afternoon

in the evening

On Saturdays, he wakes up at . . .

Writing

A Draw what you do on your day off.

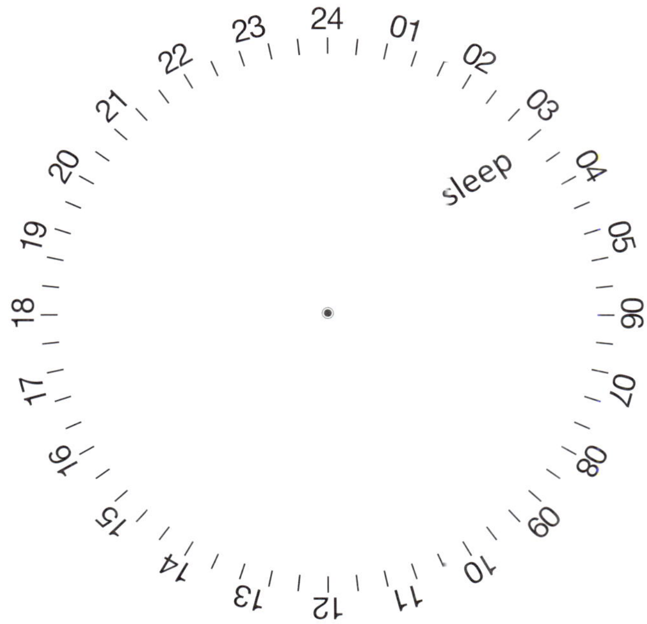

B Write about your typical day off. Then tell the class about it.

On a typical day off, I wake up at ....

....

....

Wrap-up

A Look at the pictures and complete the sentences.

1.

Ted and Alice ____________ on Saturday mornings.

2.

Elizabeth ____________ in the morning.

3.

Andy ____________ on the weekend.

B Match the questions to the correct answers.

1. Who is she?	a. Because it is fun.
2. Where do you play basketball?	b. She's my sister.
3. When do they play baseball?	c. He walks there.
4. Why do you go skiing?	d. I play basketball at the park.
5. How does he get there?	e. They play on Sunday afternoon.

C Complete the sentences with the correct seasons.

1. We go skiing in the ____________.
2. People go swimming in the ____________.
3. In the ____________, children trick-or-treat on Halloween.
4. In the ____________, people paint eggs on Easter.

D Read about Sara. Then answer the questions.

Name	Sara Ling
Job	I am a teacher. I work at a school. I teach 2nd grade.
Hobbies	I enjoy swimming in the summer. In the winter, my family loves to go skiing. I don't like the spring. It's too rainy. I love the fall because it is cool. My husband and I go for walks in the fall.
Schedule	I always get up at 6:30 a.m. I get home from work at 5:30 p.m. I go to sleep at 10:30 every night.

1. What does Sara do in the winter?
2. Who does Sara go for walks with?
3. When does Sara get home from work?
4. When does Sara go to sleep?

Unit
6 Directions

Warm-up

A What shops do you see? Put the names in the correct places.

clothes shop	coffee shop	bakery	drugstore	flower shop	pizzeria

B Look at the pictures. Which shop sells each item?

1. 
____

2. 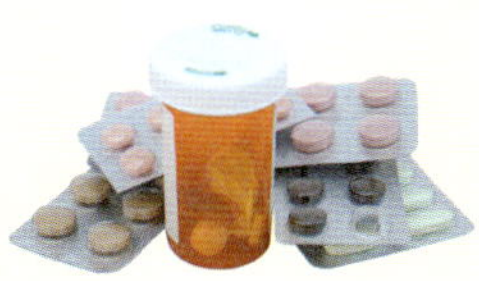
____

3. 
____

4. 
____

Where are you?

Listening

A Listen to the conversation and check the words you hear. 06-01

☐ bakery	☐ restroom	☐ restaurant	☐ drugstore
☐ bank	☐ elevator	☐ coffee shop	☐ clothes shop

B Listen again and answer the questions.

1. Where is Marcia?
   a. on the 3rd floor   b. in a clothes shop   c. in a bakery
2. What does Marcia want to do?
   a. buy a dress   b. drink a cup of coffee   c. make some bread
3. Where is the clothes shop?
   a. It is next to the elevator.
   b. It is across from the bookstore.
   c. It is between the coffee shop and the bakery.

Grammar | Prepositions of Place 2

A Let's learn about some prepositions.

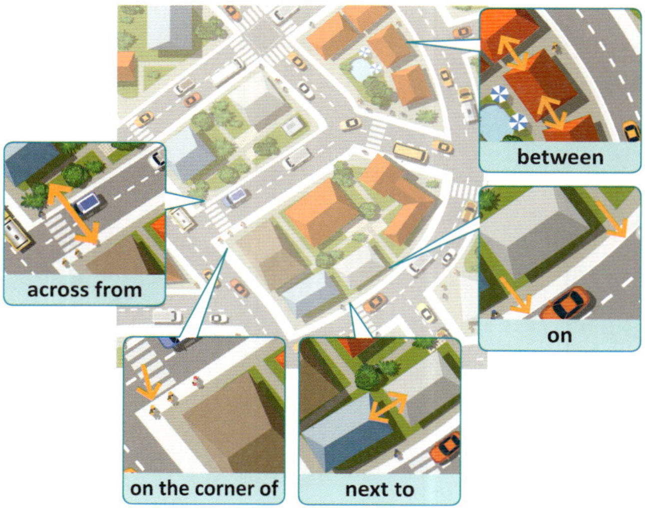

My parents and I live **in** this neighborhood.
Robert lives **on** 1st Street.
Cory's house is **next to** Christina's house.
Zoe's house is **between** the clothes shop and the coffee shop.
My house is **on the corner of** 1st Street and 3rd Avenue.
The library is **across from** my house.

B Complete the sentences with the correct prepositions.

1. Mary lives ______________ 3rd Street and 2nd Avenue.
2. Jim's house is ______________ Anne's house. They are next-door neighbors.
3. Chen is ______________ the 2nd floor. He is ______________ the restaurant now.
4. Mika lives ______________ the bakery. Every day, she walks across the street and buys some delicious bread.
5. Sam lives ______________ Jim's house and Chen's house.

I live on Green Street.

Conversation

A Listen and practice the conversation. 06-02

A Where do you live, Robert?
B I live on Green Street.
A Me, too! My house is on the corner of Green Street and 1st Street.
B Is it across from the supermarket?
A Yes, that's right. Where's your house?
B It's between the hospital and the clothes shop.
A Really? My mom works at the hospital next to your house. She's a doctor.

B Look at the map and answer the questions.

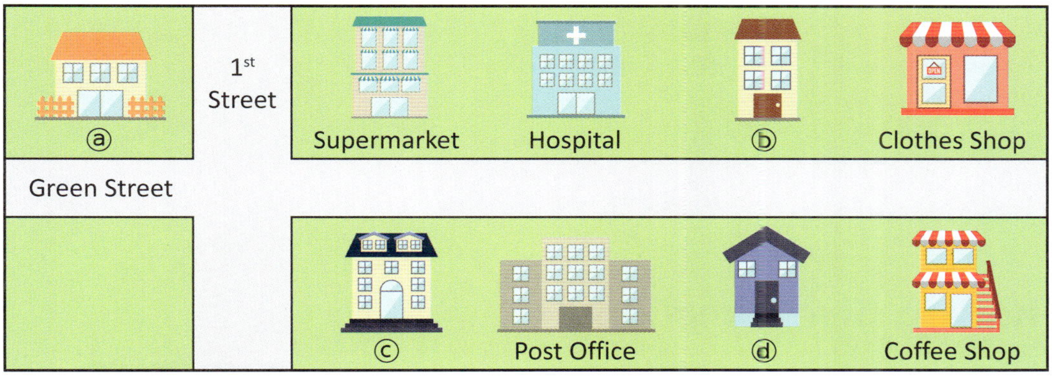

1. On which street do the speakers live?
2. Which house is the woman's house?
3. Which house is the man's house?
4. Where does the woman's mom work?

Pair Work Look at the map. Then ask your partner where each building is.

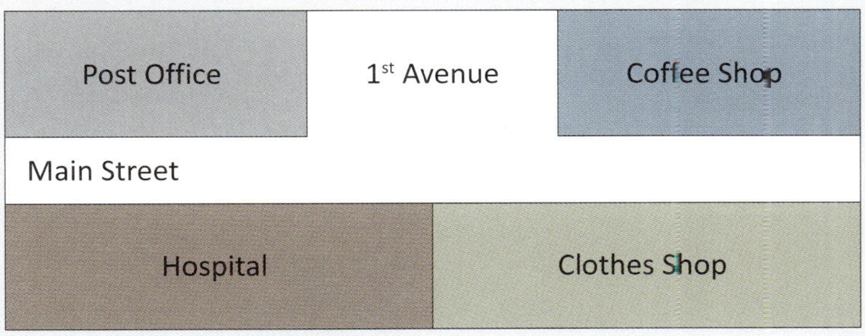

A Where is the post office?
B It is on the corner of 1st Avenue and Main Street.

How do I get to the park?

Listening

A Listen to the conversation and choose True or False. 06-03

1. The man wants to find the library. [True / False]
2. The woman doesn't live in the area. [True / False]
3. The post office is across from the school. [True / False]

B Listen again. Where does the woman want to go?

		1.	School	2.
▶ HERE				1st Street
3.		Police Station	4.	

TIPS & TIPS Asking for Directions

Excuse me. Where is the school?
Pardon me, sir. How do [can] I get to the park?

Vocabulary | How to Give Directions

Go [Walk] straight on Main Street.
Go [Walk] down Main Street.

Turn right on 2nd Street.
Take a right on 2nd Street.

Turn left on Central Avenue.
Take a left on Central Avenue.

Pair Work Look at the map of the train station. Then ask your partner where the bookstore, the clothes shop, the store, and the gate are.

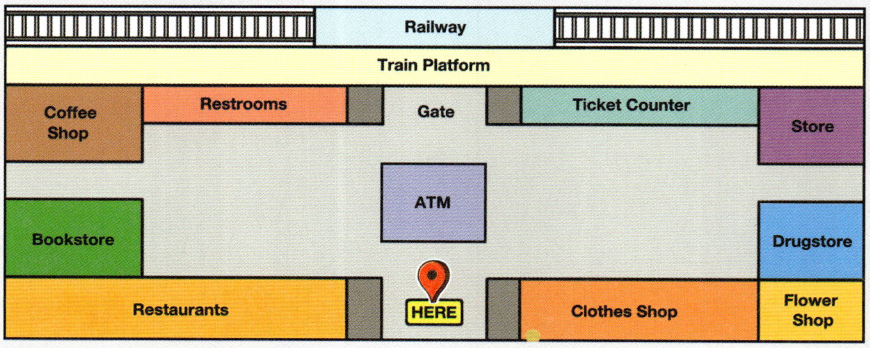

A How do you get to the bookstore?
B Go straight and turn left at the ATM. The bookstore is next to the restaurant.

City Map

A Where do the people want to go? Put the correct names on the map.

B Start from **Here** on the map above. Follow each of the directions. Which shop do you find on the map?

1.

____

2.

____

3.

____

Around Town

Megan's Neighborhood

A Listen to Megan's talk. Then answer the questions. 06-04

1. When is Megan busy?
   a. every Monday morning
   b. on weekdays
   c. on weekends
2. Check the four places Megan goes on the map.

B Listen to Samantha's talk. Then answer the questions.

1. Where is Samantha? Find her location on the map.
2. Samantha tries to use her GPS to find Pineville Burgers. Which directions are correct?
   a. Go straight on 2nd Avenue for one block. Turn right on Lake Street. Pineville Burgers is on the right.
   b. Go straight on 2nd Avenue for two blocks. Turn right on Oak Street. Pineville Burgers is on the left.

C Look at the online post. Then answer the questions.

Pet Palace
May 20

Attention!

*Pet Palace is **now** in a **new** location.*

Find us **at 124 Oak Street across from the train station.**

We have free treats for the first 100 lucky animals.

Like · Comment · Share

52 people like this.

View all 39 comments.

Write a comment . . .

1. Find and circle the new Pet Palace on the map.
2. These are the directions from the old place to the new place. Which one is correct?
   a. From the Pine Street entrance, go down Pine Street for three blocks. Then turn left. The new pet shop is across from the grocery store.
   b. From the 1st Avenue entrance, go down one block on 1st Avenue and turn left on Pine Street. Go straight two blocks and turn right on 3rd Avenue. Go down two blocks. The new pet shop is on 3rd Avenue and Oak Street.

Pair Work

Find or draw a map of your city. Choose one place on the map. Then ask your partner for directions.

A I am at the post office. How can I get there?

B Go down 1st Avenue. Turn left on Oak Street. Walk two blocks. It is on your left.

Popular Places to Visit

Reading

Read the map of Fisherman's Wharf in San Francisco. 06-05

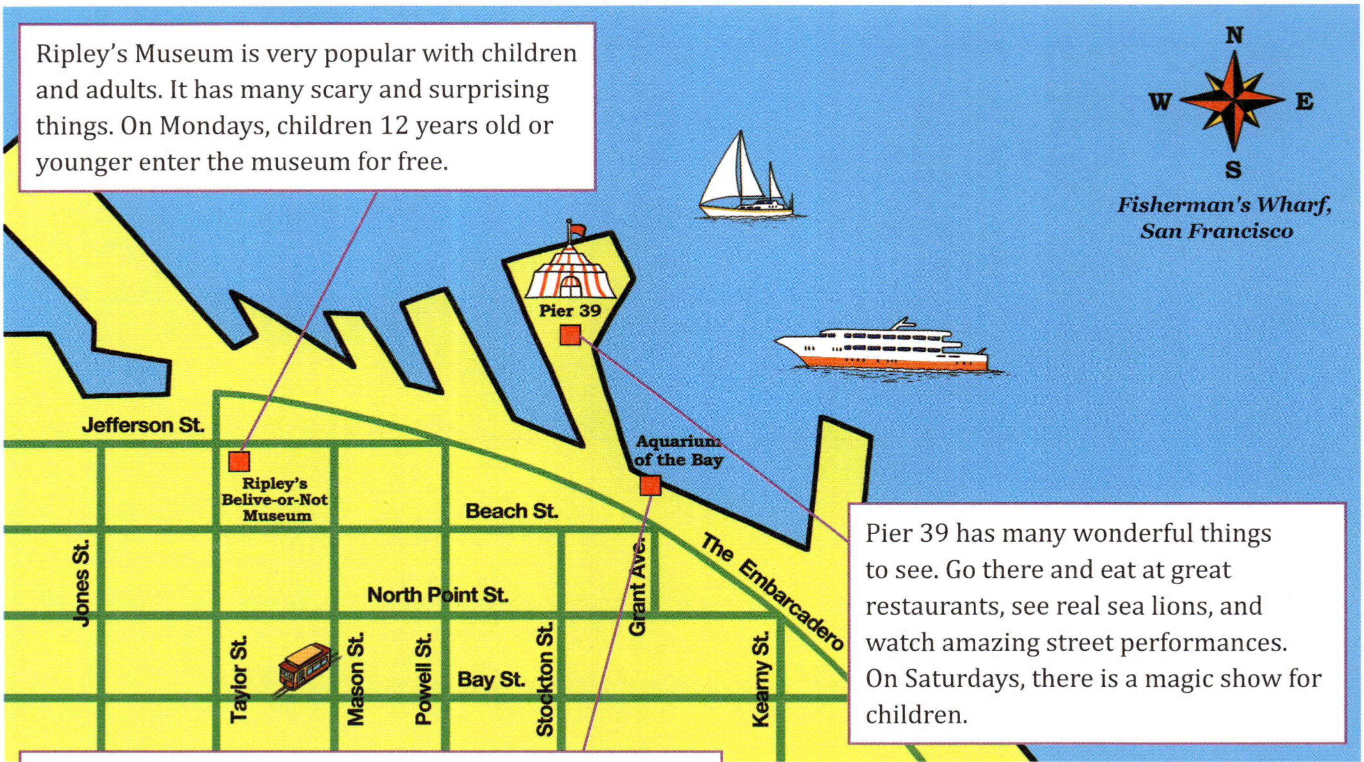

Ripley's Museum is very popular with children and adults. It has many scary and surprising things. On Mondays, children 12 years old or younger enter the museum for free.

Pier 39 has many wonderful things to see. Go there and eat at great restaurants, see real sea lions, and watch amazing street performances. On Saturdays, there is a magic show for children.

At Aquarium of the Bay, people learn about many kinds of sea creatures, including tropical fish, dolphins, and sharks. On Fridays, Sparky the Seal performs free shows at 1:00 p.m. and 3:00 p.m. Children love the seal show!

Comprehension Check Answer the questions about Fisherman's Wharf.

1. Which place is popular with adults and children?
2. What does Ripley's Museum have?
3. Who doesn't pay at Ripley's Museum on Mondays?
4. Which place has nice restaurants and street performances?
5. What kind of show is there on Saturdays on Pier 39?
6. When are there free shows at Aquarium of the Bay?

Pair Work

Imagine you and your partner are at Fisherman's Wharf. Practice giving directions.

A How do we get from Ripley's Museum to Pier 39?

B The map says to go straight on Jefferson Street. Then turn right on Embarcadero. Oh, there it is!

Class Activity

A Ask three students about the most popular place in their city.

	Name:	Name:	Name:
What's the most popular place in your city?			
Where is it?			
How do you get there?			
What do people do there?			
Do you like the place?			
Why or why not?			

B Write about one student's place.

Wrap-up

A Look at the map. Then complete the sentences with the correct prepositions.

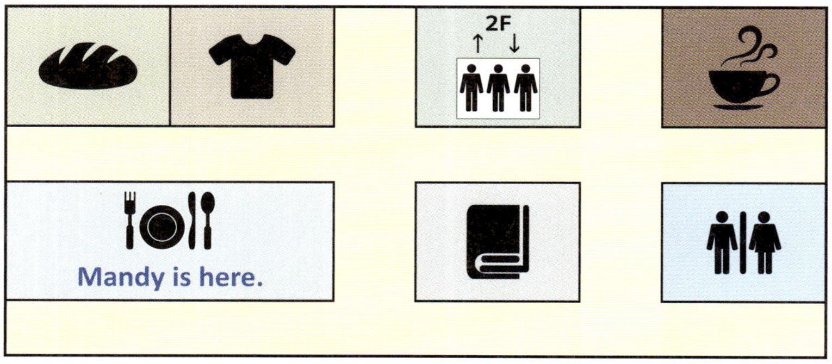

1. Where is Mandy? - She's ______________ the 2nd floor. She is ______________ the restaurant.
2. Where's the bookstore? - It's ______________ the restrooms and the restaurant.
3. Where's the clothes shop? - It's ______________ the bakery.

B Look at the GPS information. Then complete the directions.

From 188 Mary Street to 65 Campbell Street

4 min (152m)
Via 1st St. and Oat St.

188 Mary Street

on 1st Street 13m	Go down one block on ____________.
on Oak Street 61m	____________ on Oak Street. Go straight two blocks.
on Campbell Street 78m	____________ on Campbell Street. Go straight two blocks.
65 Campbell Street	It is on ______________ of Campbell Street and Main Street.

C Draw a floor map of the building your classroom is in. Then answer the questions.

1. Which floor is your classroom on?
2. Where is the elevator, or where are the stairs?
3. How do you get to your classroom from the elevator or stairs?
4. A guest is in the main entrance of your school building. Give him or her directions to your classroom.

Unit 7

Shopping

Warm-up

A Look at the pictures. Are the shoppers in the right shops? Where should they go?

B Look at the pictures again. What shops are they? Complete the sentences.

1. It is . . .
2. The place looks like . . .
3. The man is in . . .
4. The woman works at . . .

How much is this umbrella?

Conversation

Listen and practice the conversation. 07-01

A Can I help you?
B Yes, please. How much is this umbrella?
A It's $12.00.
B How much are these rain boots?
A They are $56.99.
B Thanks.

Prices

99¢ = ninety-nine cents
$35 = thirty-five dollars
$35.99 = thirty-five dollars and ninety-nine cents OR thirty-five ninety-nine
$352.50 = three hundred and fifty-two dollars and fifty cents OR three hundred fifty-two fifty

Q. What is the currency in your country?

Pair Work Look at the pictures. Then ask and answer questions about the prices with your partner.

A How much are the sunglasses?
B They are $128.

Listening

Listen to the conversations and choose the correct prices. 07-02

1. a. $17.46 b. $70.46
2. a. $49.99 b. $99.49
3. a. $80.50 b. $18.50
4. a. $40.18 b. $14.80

TIPS & TIPS Currencies

$ = USD = dollar (CAD: Canadian dollar, AUD: Australian dollar)

€ = EUR = euro £ = GBP = pound

¥ = JPY = yen ¥ = CNY = yuan ₩ = KRW = won

Vocabulary | Money

A Let's learn about various payment methods.

credit card

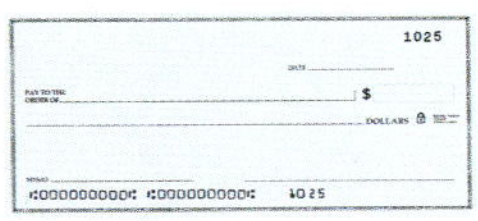

check / cheque

cash

bill / note

coin

* Cash typically means bills and coins.

B Look at the pictures and complete the sentences with the correct words.

1.

I am sorry. We don't take ____________.

2.

Yes, we accept ____________.

3.

I only take ____________.

4.

Put a 25-cent ____________ here.

Pair Work

Choose three items you have. Then sell and buy the items with your partner.

A How much is this hat?
B It's $16.50.
A Do you take credit cards?
B I'm sorry, but we only accept cash.

A How much is this computer?
B It's $980.00.
A Do you take credit cards?
B Of course, we do.

They are in the Electronics Department.

Conversation

Listen and practice the conversation. 07-03

Attention, shoppers! Big sale! Everything is 50% off.

A Excuse me. Do you have cell phones?
B Yes, we do. They are in the Electronics Department.
A Do you sell headphones, too?
B Yes. They are in the same section.
A Thanks.

Vocabulary | Departments in a Shopping Mall

A Put the numbers in the correct places.

1. MP3 player	2. vitamins	3. shoes	4. sun cream
5. refrigerator	6. summer dresses	7. dishwasher	8. cell phones

Electronics

[ ] [ ]

Clothing & Shoes

[ ] [ ]

Home Appliances

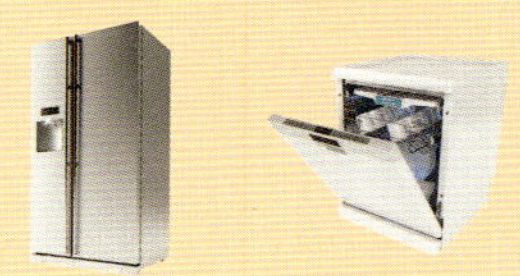

[ ] [ ]

Health & Beauty

[ ] [ ]

B Complete the conversations with the correct departments.

1. A Where are men's jeans?
   B They're in the ______________________.
2. A Do you have washing machines?
   B They're in the ______________________.
3. A Are there any sandals here?
   B Yes, they're in ______________________.

How to Ask If a Store Has an Item

Do you have pens?
Do you sell sunglasses?
Where can I find children's books?
Is there a Clothing Department in this store?

Do you have it in black?

Conversation

Listen and practice the conversation. 07-04

A Excuse me. Do you have this jacket in black?
B Let me check . . . Yes, we do.
A How much is it?
B It's $28.59.
A Great. I would like a medium, please.
B Sure. Here you go.
A Here's $30.00.
B And here are your change and receipt.

TIPS & TIPS Sizes

XS = extra small	S = small	M = medium
L = large	XL = extra large	XXL = double extra large

I want a small.
Do you have a large-sized shirt?
I would like these pants in size 30.

Pair Work Buy these items from your partner. Ask for different sizes and colors.

A I like this shirt. Do you have it in black?
B I'm sorry, but we only have it in green, yellow, blue, and red.

A I like these pants. Do you have them in 32?
B Yes, we do.
A How much are they?
B They are $45.
A Here's $50.
B And here's your change.

I'd like to exchange this shirt.

Conversation

Listen and practice the conversation. 07-05

A Hello. I'd like to exchange this shirt.
B Is something wrong with it?
A It's too small around the neck.
B What size is it?
A It's a large.
B What size would you like?
A An extra-large, please.
B Here you are.

* I'd = I would

How to Ask about a Problem

Is there a problem?
Is something wrong with the hat?
What's wrong with the jeans?
What seems to be the problem?

Grammar | *So and Too*

A Let's learn the difference between *so* and *too*.

· so
· very

This pumpkin is **so big**.
It is **very big**.

· too
· not ~ enough

These shoes are **too big**.
They are **not small enough**.

B Look at the pictures and choose the correct sentences.

1.

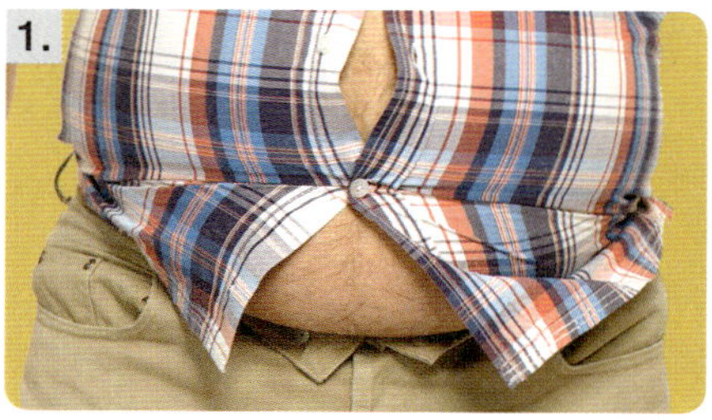

☐ This shirt is so big.
☐ This shirt is too small.

2.

☐ This car is so fast.
☐ This car is not fast enough.

3.

☐ This bag is too expensive.
☐ This bag is very cheap.

I want to return it.

Conversation

Listen and practice the conversation. 07-06

A I don't want this sweater. It is too small.
B Would you like to exchange it?
A No, I want to return it.
B Sure. Do you have the receipt?
A Here it is.
B Here's your money back.

How to Say You Want Your Money Back

I want to return this bag.
I would like a refund for these sunglasses.
Can I get a refund for this watch?

Listening

Listen to the conversations and choose the correct words. 07-07

1.

He wants to (exchange / return) it.
He thinks it is too (expensive / big).

2.

She wants to (exchange / return) them.
She doesn't like the (style / color).

3.

She would like to (exchange / return) it.
She thinks it is not (short / big) enough.

Group Work Choose one student to be the shopkeeper. The other group members are shoppers. Then exchange or return the items from the list below.

Clothes & Shoes	Electronics	Health & Beauty
shirts, pants, coats, boots . . .	computers, cell phones, headphones, speakers . . .	vitamins, body lotion, shampoo, sun cream . . .

A I'd like to return these shoes.
B What's the matter with them?
A They're too big.
B Oh, I see.

A I'd like to exchange this cell phone.
B What's wrong with it?
A The screen is too small.
B Okay.

Shopping Habits

Reading

Read the newspaper column. 07-08

CAPITAL CITY NEWSPAPER

Dr. Sarah's Advice

Dear Dr. Sarah,

My wife Kathy loves to go shopping at department stores and malls, but I hate going shopping. I prefer to do all my shopping online. Kathy asks me to go shopping with her, but I say no. Then we argue. Online shopping is so much better than shopping at stores. The prices for clothes and electronics are so much cheaper online. They also bring the packages right to your front door. You don't have to move an inch. My wife and I argue about this issue often, so I thought I would ask you for your advice. What should I do, Dr. Sarah? Please help!

Ken K.

Dear Ken,

It is normal for couples to disagree and argue about things. But in these situations, it is helpful to consider the other person's side, too. For example, shopping online is easier, but sometimes the clothes you buy don't fit, so you have to send them back or lose your money. At a department store, you can try clothes on, so you know they fit right. In addition, sitting in front of a computer all day isn't very healthy. Getting out of the house and moving around are good for your heart. I think you and Kathy need an activity you both enjoy. Why don't you go hiking, ride bikes, or go to the beach? Doing something together as a couple will bring you closer together.

Dr. Sarah

Comprehension Check Answer the questions about the column.

1. What is the couple's problem?
2. Where does Kathy prefer to shop? How about Ken?
3. Why does Ken like shopping online?
4. What does Dr. Sarah say about online shopping?
5. What is Dr. Sarah's advice for the couple?

Speaking

Do you like shopping online or offline? Why?

Listening

A Listen to three women talking about their favorite shops. Then write the names Patty, Janet, and Mindy in the correct places. 07-09

1. 

____

2. 

____

3. 

____

B Listen again and choose the correct words.

1. Patty's favorite shop is right next to her ______________.
   a. work b. school c. home
2. The Rainbow Café is ______________.
   a. quiet b. dirty c. small
3. The clothes at Janet's favorite shop are a little ______________.
   a. old b. cheap c. expensive
4. Mindy's favorite shop is a ______________.
   a. restaurant b. bookstore c. bakery
5. Mindy goes to her favorite shop every ______________.
   a. Monday b. Thursday c. Sunday

Writing

Complete the table with your own information. Then write a short essay about your favorite shop.

What is your favorite shop?	Where is it?	What does it sell?	How often do you go there?

My favorite shop is . . .

Wrap-up

A Imagine you are a salesperson. Say how much each item is.

1. 
$49.99

2. 
$218.80

3. 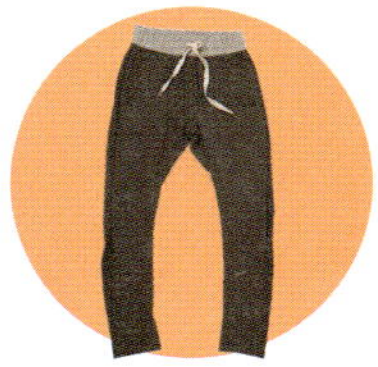
$15.50

4. 
$330.00

This hat is forty-nine dollars and ninety-nine cents. / This hat is forty-nine ninety-nine.

B Put the words in the correct places.

Home Appliances	headphones	Pharmacy & Health	blue jeans

1. A Excuse me. Do you sell ____________________?
   B Yes, they're in the Electronics Department.
2. A Pardon me. Where's the skin lotion?
   B It's in ____________________.
3. A I want to buy a washing machine. Where is the ____________________ Department?
   B It's over there. It's next to the Electronics Department.
4. A I want to buy some ____________________. Where do I find them?
   B Men's Clothing is on the 3rd floor.

C Look at the pictures and complete the conversations with the correct words.

1. 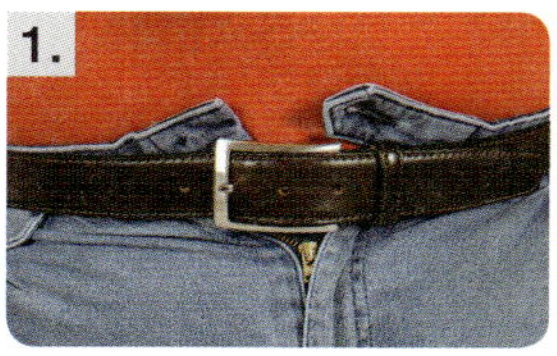

A I'd like to __________ these jeans.
B What is the problem with them?
A They are too __________. These are size 32, but I need 36.
B Okay, here is a pair of size 36 jeans.

2. 

A I'd like to __________ this bag.
B What's wrong with it?
A It's too __________.
B Would you like to see some other bags?
A No, I just want my money back.

D Visit an online clothes shop. Then answer the questions.

1. What is today's deal? How much is it?
2. What kinds of clothes do you want to buy? In what color and size do you want them?

Unit
8
Food

Warm-up

A What does she need to buy? Read the shopping list. Then find the items in the picture.

Shopping List

1. beef
2. cheese
3. apples
4. bread
5. tomatoes

B Look at the five food categories. Then write each food item from the shopping list above in the correct places.

1.

vegetables

____

2.

fruit

____

3.

grain

____

4.

dairy

____

5.

meat & protein

____

Is there any milk in the refrigerator?

Conversation

Listen and practice the conversation. 08-01

A I want some pasta for dinner.
B Let's make some then. Is there any milk in the refrigerator?
A No, there isn't. But there are some tomatoes. How about making tomato pasta?
B Sure. Is there any bread?
A There's some on the table.
B Oh, good. Is the large pot clean?
A Yes. Here it is . . . Oh, wait. Oh, no!
B What?
A There isn't any pasta.

Grammar | *Some* and *Any*

A Let's learn about *some* and *any*.

	some	any	
Positive	There is **some** water. He has **some** pencils.	There isn't **any** cheese. She never drinks **any** alcohol.	***Negative***
Offers	Would you like **some** coffee?	Do you have **any** money?	***Question***
		If you have **any** questions, please let me know.	with ***if***

B Choose *some* or *any*.

1. There isn't (some / any) sugar in the cabinet.
2. There are (some / any) people in the library.
3. I am so tired. I need (some / any) rest.
4. A Is there (any / some) rice in the cupboard?
   B No, there isn't (any / some).
5. A Do you have (some / any) bread?
   B No, I don't have (some / any).
6. There is (any / some) water in the cup.
7. A Would you like (some / any) iced tea?
   B Yes, I would like (some / any).
8. If there is (some / any) news, please call me.

Listening

A Listen to the conversation and answer the questions. 08-02

1. What does the man want to eat?
   a. potato chips b. fish and chips c. potato salad

2. What is in the fridge?
   a. potato chips b. orange juice c. onions

* fridgere = frigerator

B Listen again and choose True or False.

1. The man doesn't see any potato chips in the cupboard. [True / False]
2. There isn't any yogurt in the refrigerator. [True / False]
3. There is some orange juice in the refrigerator. [True / False]
4. The yogurt is on the middle shelf. [True / False]

Pair Work

Look at the picture. Are these food items in the cupboard? Ask and answer the questions with your partner.

cheese	apples	milk	pasta
bananas	potatoes	salt	cans of tuna

A Is there any cheese in the cupboard?
B No, there isn't any (cheese).

A Are there any apples in the cupboard?
B Yes, there are some (apples).

Class Activity

Ask three classmates what they have in their fridges. Then answer the questions from the results of the survey.

What's in your fridge?		
Name:	Name:	Name:

1. Who has the most food items in his or her fridge?
2. What is the most common food item?
3. What food items from the survey do you NOT have in your fridge?

I need a box of cereal.

Conversation

Listen and practice the conversation. 08-03

A What do we need?
B Well, first, I want some bananas for breakfast.
A Oh, right. And I need a box of cereal . . . And these!
B Two cans of soda? You know you eat too much sugar. Have some bananas with me instead.
A No! I love these! Don't you eat any sweet foods?
B Well, there is a bar of chocolate in the cart.
A See!
B But I don't eat it for breakfast.

Vocabulary | Measure Words

a box of cereal

a can of soda

a bar of chocolate

a bag of rice

a jar of jam

a spoon of honey

a cup of coffee

a bottle of water

a carton of milk

a dozen eggs = 12 eggs

Listening

A Listen to the conversation and answer the questions. 08-04

1. What is for dinner?
   a. rice soup b. pork chops c. fried eggs
2. Where are the speakers?
   a. at home b. at a restaurant c. at a grocery store

B Listen again. Then check the correct items on the shopping list.

Shopping List

- ☐ two cans of tuna fish
- ☐ three cans of tuna fish
- ☐ six eggs
- ☐ twelve eggs
- ☐ a bag of rice
- ☐ two bags of rice

Reading

Read Mila's text messages with Anthony. 08-05

●●○○○ DWT 2:00 PM

< Messages **Anthony** Contact

Anthony, what do you want for tonight's dinner party? It's for our new roommate. I want something good. I want him to really like us.

Mila, I have a great idea. Let's order from the Burger Palace I always eat dinner there. It's cheap and delicious. How about cheeseburgers and French fries? Maybe with some beer? Everyone loves fast food!

I don't! Junk food? For the new roommate? It's a terrible idea!

Okay, okay. Relax, scary Mila.

I think a healthy meal is the best choice. I want to cook some homemade beef stew. Buy some potatoes, onions, and carrots. We have beef in the fridge.

And beer! All right, beef stew for tonight then.

iMessage Send

Comprehension Check Answer the questions about the text messages.

1. What does Anthony typically eat for dinner?
2. Why does Anthony eat fast food? Give two reasons.
3. What does Mila think of Anthony's dinner idea?
4. What does Mila want to cook for dinner?
5. What does Anthony need to buy?

Speaking

What is your favorite everyday food? Why do you like it?

Sandwiches are my favorite food. I like them because they are easy to find. They are also cheap.

I'd like to order a hamburger.

Conversation

Listen and practice the conversation. 08-06

A Welcome to Burger Palace. How may I help you?

B Yes, I'd like to order a number two meal with a diet soda, please.

A So that's a hamburger, French fries, and a diet soda. Is that right?

B Yes. That's correct.

A Is that for here or to go?

B For here.

A Your total is $6.15.

B Here's $10.00.

A And here's your change. Next!

* a soda = a can of soda   a coffee = a cup of coffee

Listening

A Listen to the conversation. Then choose the food items the speaker orders. 08-07

1. 
2. 
3. 
4. 
5. 
6. 
7. 
8. 
9. 
10. 

B Listen again and answer the questions.

1. How many hamburgers does the speaker want?
   a. 1   b. 2   c. 3

2. What is the total price of the order?
   a. $25.97   b. $27.59   c. $29.57

Pair Work

Practice the conversation with your partner.
Use the information from the menu.

A How may I help you?

B Yes, I'd like a large pizza with one topping, please.

A What topping would you like?

B Olives, please.

A Is that for here or to go?

B For here.

A Your total is $18.99.

Little Bingo's Pizzeria

Large pizza with one topping	$18.99
Medium pizza with one topping	$9.99
Extra topping	$2.00

Extra topping choices: pepperoni, sausage, green peppers, olives, pineapple, onions

I'd like the chicken lunch, please.

Conversation

Listen and practice the conversation. 08-08

A Are you ready to order?

B Yes. I'd like the chicken lunch, please.

A Sure. Would you like it with a baked potato or French fries?

B A baked potato, please.

A Would you like something to drink?

B Yes. I'd like a cup of coffee.

A Okay. That's the chicken lunch with a baked potato and a cup of coffee.

Listening

Le Café

Sandwiches	
Ham Sandwich	5.99
Cheese Sandwich	4.99
Ham & Cheese	7.00
Chicken Sandwich	5.50
Fish Sandwich	5.50
Turkey Club	6.50

Soups	
Chicken Noodle Soup	3 99
Tomato Basil Soup	4 99
Chili with Corn	5 50
Clam Chowder	6 25
Mushroom Soup	5 90
Beef Stew	6 00

Drinks	
Soda	1.00
Espresso	2.00
Americano	3.00
Latte	3.50
Iced Tea	3.50
Beer	4.00

A Listen to the talk. What is today's special at Le Café? 08-09

B Listen to the conversations in Le Café. Then circle the answers on the menu.

1. Which sandwich does the speaker want?
2. Which soup does the speaker want?
3. Which drink does the speaker want?

C Imagine that you are in Le Café. Order a meal under $10.

I would like the chicken sandwich and a beer, please.

A Recipe for Weekday Super Pizza

Reading

A Read a post on a blog. 08-10

Marta's Cooking Corner

Weekday Super Pizza

Who wants to cook on weekdays? Not me! I just want to come home, eat dinner, and then sleep! I know there are more people like me out there. So this week, I want to share this great recipe. It is easy and quick but very delicious. I call it Weekday Super Pizza! You only need 4 ingredients to make this delicious pizza. Here they are:

1 large *pita bread*

some *ham*

2 cups *of fresh mozzarella cheese*

1 can *of pineapple*

Let's get ready. Heat the oven to 220 degrees Celsius. Cut the ham into small pieces. Open the can of pineapple and throw out the juice. Now, start cooking. First, put the pita bread on the baking pan. Second, put the ham on top. Next, cover the pita with mozzarella cheese. After that, put on some pineapple. Finally, put the pan in the oven. And bake it for about 10 minutes. That's it! Now you have a hot, cheesy, delicious pizza to enjoy.

Hi! I am Marta.
I am not a cook!
I just enjoy cooking and sharing easy recepies.

Follow me on

- Friendbook
- Chit-chatter
- Pictureshare

Comprehension Check Complete the sentences with the correct words.

1. Marta likes ______________.
2. This recipe is to make a ______________.
3. A person needs ______________ ingredients to make this pizza.
4. A person needs to heat an oven to ______________ degrees Celsius.
5. It takes about 10 minutes to ______________ this pizza.

B Complete the directions of the recipe.

Directions

______________, put the large pita on the baking pan.
Second, put the ______________ on top.
Next, cover the pita with ______________.
After that, add some ______________.
______________, bake the pita for 10 minutes.

Writing

A Look at the picture and answer the questions.

1. What do you see? Find these fruits and vegetables.

lettuce	corn	apple
tomato	onion	lemon

2. Imagine you want to make a salad. What do you want in your salad? Choose from the picture.
3. Is there anything else you want to add to your salad? What are they?

B Write a recipe for your salad.

My Salad: ____________________

Ingredients:

Directions:

Presentation

Share your salad recipe with the class.

Wrap-up

A Read the conversations and choose *some* or *any*.

1. A Barbara, do we have (some / any) juice in the fridge?
   B Yes. There's (some / any) on the middle shelf.
2. A We don't have (some / any) apples on the table.
   B No, we don't have (some / any).
3. A Here. Have (some / any) bread.
   B Thanks. Is there (some / any) water, too?

B Look at the picture. Then say what items are in the shopping bag.

1. *There is* ....
2. ....
3. ....
4. ....
5. ....

C Look at the menu. Then order one burger, one side dish, and one drink.

LUNCH MENU

Burgers		Sides		Drinks	
Hamburger	4.99	French Fries	1.99	Soda	1.99
Cheeseburger	4.99	Onion Ring	1.99	Orange Juice	1.49
Chicken Burger	4.49	Garden Salad	2.99	Coffee	2.49
Fish Burger	4.99				

D Choose one simple dish you like. Say what ingredients you need and how to make it. Use *first*, *second*, *next*, *after that*, and *last*.

Body and Health

Warm-up

Look at the pictures. Then write the names of the body parts in the correct places.

I am just resting.

Conversation

Listen and practice the conversation. 09-01

A Hello.

B Jim, what are you doing? Are you still sleeping? You're late for work!

A No, I'm not sleeping. I'm not feeling well today.

B Are you sick?

A Yeah.

B What's wrong?

A I have a headache, a cough, and a fever. So I'm just resting at home.

B Oh, you have the flu. I am sorry to hear that. Get better soon.

Vocabulary | Common Illnesses and Symptoms

A Let's learn about common illnesses and symptoms.

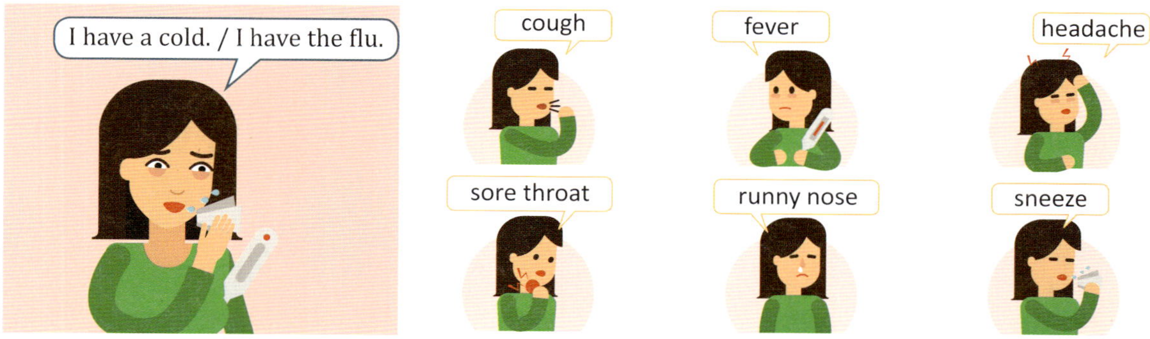

* N + **ache**: head**ache**, tooth**ache**, back**ache**, stomach**ache**
sore + N: **sore** throat, **sore** muscles

B Complete the sentences with the correct words.

1. Do you have any tissues? I have a ____________.
2. The boy's body temperature is 39℃. He has a ____________.
3. Kelly needs to see a dentist. She has a ____________.
4. This tea is good for a ____________.
5. A Why are you wearing a mask?
   B I have a ____________. I am sneezing a lot.
6. A Why are you holding your head?
   B I have a ____________.

Grammar | Present Continuous Tense

A Let's learn about the present continuous tense.

I **am** watch**ing** TV. We **are** hav**ing** dinner.	She **isn't** study**ing** English. You **aren't** do**ing** well.	**Is** Jamie play**ing** soccer? **Are** they clean**ing** the house?

B Complete the sentences by using the present continuous tense.

1. She ______________ a movie. (watch)
2. They ______________ dinner. (eat)
3. I ______________ English. (not / study)
4. We ____________ to music. (listen)
5. A Are you playing soccer?
   B No, ______________. I ______________ football. (play)
6. He ______________. (not / swim)
7. It ______________ today. (rain)

Listening

A Listen to the phone conversations and choose True or False. 09-02

1. Mandy is talking with her mom. [True / False]
2. Mandy has a bad toothache. [True / False]
3. Jake is drinking tea. [True / False]
4. Jake has a sore back. [True / False]

B Listen to the phone conversations and choose the correct words.

1.

a. The man has (a cold / the flu).
b. The man is going (home / to work) right now.

2.

a. The woman's (arm / leg) hurts.
b. The woman is (waiting for / meeting with) the doctor now.

I feel terrible.

Conversation

Listen and practice the conversation. 09-03

A Doctor, I feel terrible. I'm tired all the time.
B Why are you so tired?
A I don't know. I'm busy all day at work. But I don't sleep very well at night.
B How many cups of coffee do you drink in a day?
A Not many. About 4 or 5 cups. Is that too many?
B Of course it is! Don't drink so much coffee.
A Okay. Anything else?
B Do some exercise. It helps you sleep better.

Grammar | Imperatives

A Let's learn about imperatives.

Get better soon.	**Don't drink** too much coffee.
Read more books.	**Don't work** too hard.
Be happy.	**Don't be** late.

B Look at the pictures. Then complete the sentences by using imperatives.

1.

______ too much junk food. (not / eat) Eat fruit instead.

2.

______. (not / smoke) It is not good for your health.

3.

______ late. (not / stay up) Go to bed early.

4.

Be active. ______ daily. (exercise)

5.

______ more time with your family and friends. (spend)

6.

Think about something good. ______ positive. (be)

Listening

A Listen to the conversations. Then write the problems the speakers have. 09-04

1. Sarah has ______________________.
2. Chen has ______________________.
3. James has ______________________.
4. Amanda has ______________________.

B Listen to the doctor's advice for Lynn. Then choose the correct advice.

	Do	Don't	Doctor's Advice
1			Take some pills.
2.			Drink more water, coffee, and alcohol.
3.			Stay in bed and be lazy.
4.			Don't try to do too much.

Speaking

Imagine that the people in the picture are your patients. Give some advice to each person.

A Doctor, I have a cold.

B Oh, I am sorry to hear that. Take these pills.

This is my usual breakfast.

Conversation

Listen and practice the conversation. 09-05

A Wow. You have a lot of food, Kevin. Are you that hungry?
B Oh, this is normal for me. I like a big breakfast.
A How often do you eat a breakfast like this?
B About 4 or 5 times a week, I guess. How about you?
A Almost never. I don't have any energy in the morning.
B Here. Have some of my breakfast. You probably don't have any energy because you're always hungry.
A Hmm. Maybe you're right. Thanks.

The Number of Times

Let's learn about the number of times.

I go shopping **once** a week.

They do yoga **twice** a week.

He studies English **three times** a week.

Sunny goes swimming **four times** a week.

The students go to school **five times** a week.

	M	T	W	T	F	S	S
shopping						o	
yoga		o		o			
English	o		o		o		
swimming		o		o		o	o
school	o	o	o	o	o		

Pair Work

Practice the conversations with your partner.

A How many times a week do you drink coffee?
B I drink coffee five times a week.

A How often do Mike and Molly watch movies?
B They watch movies once a month.

Listening

A Listen to the radio broadcast. Then choose the correct advice from the doctor. 09-06

1. Eat too little.
2. Drink more fruit juice.
3. Drink enough water.
4. Exercise.
5. Use the stairs.
6. Drive every day.
7. Think positively.

B Listen again. According to Dr. Barns, how often do you need to do these activities below?

1. Eat fruits and vegetables.
   a. once a day b. twice a day c. three times or more a day
2. Don't use your car.
   a. once a day b. once a week c. once a month

Listening

A Listen to the conversation and choose True or False. 09-07

1. Angela thinks Tom looks great. [True / False]
2. Tom is trying to give Angela some advice on losing weight. [True / False]

B Listen again and answer the questions.

1. What is Tom doing these days?
   a. He is exercising a lot.
   b. He is taking Angela's yoga class.
   c. He is swimming every day.
2. What kinds of exercise is Tom doing? Choose two.
   a. running
   b. swimming
   c. yoga
3. What is true about Tom?
   a. He is trying to gain weight.
   b. He is doing yoga three times a week.
   c. He is not eating snacks at all.

Class Activity

A Survey the class. Find out how often the other students do the activities in the table.

	1~3 times a week	4~5 times a week	every day
eat breakfast			
exercise			
eat salad for a meal			
sleep for 8 hours			
dream			

A How often do you eat breakfast each week? / How many times a week do you eat breakfast?
B I eat breakfast 3 or 4 times a week.

B Answer the questions about the survey.

1. Which activity do the students do the most often?
2. Which activity do the students do the least often?

Old but Healthy

Reading

Read the article from a magazine. 09-08

As I travel around the world, I meet all kinds of interesting people. I learn about their cultures and lifestyles. Okinawa, Japan, is an amazing place. It has more people 100 years old or older than any other place in the world. Why are they so healthy? What is their secret? I talked to one of them recently. This is Machiko. She is 102 years old. She was kind enough to let me ask her some questions.

Healthy Life (HL): Can you tell me about your lifestyle, Machiko?

Machiko (M): Yes, I can. One of the most important things to me is my garden. I love working in my garden. I grow fruits and vegetables. I cook with the fruits and vegetables I grow. I make food for my friends, family, and myself.

HL: Tell me about the food you eat.

M: I never eat junk food. I make vegetable dishes, and I eat them with rice. I also eat a lot of tofu. I usually buy it at the market. I eat fish once in a while.

HL: What else do you do? Do you see your family and friends often?

M: My granddaughter lives with me. She helps me in my garden. I am very close to her. But my friends are very old. I only see them once or twice a month.

HL: You enjoy outdoor activities, eat well, and stay close to your family and friends. Is there anything else you do to live a long and healthy life?

M: Yes. I try to think positively. A positive mind is better than the best medicine.

HL: Thank you so much, Machiko.

M: You're welcome. It was my pleasure.

Comprehension Check **Answer the questions about the article.**

1. How old is Machiko?
2. What activity is very important to Machiko?
3. Who does Machiko live with?
4. How often does Machiko visit her friends?
5. What does Machiko do to live a long healthy life?

Speaking

What do you do to live a long and healthy life? Say three healthy habits you have.

I like eating vegetables. I try to walk up the stairs. I do yoga three times a week.

How healthy are you?

A Read each question in the table. Then check **Yes** or **No** based on your own information.

	How healthy are you?	Yes	No
1	Do you try not to eat meat too often?		
2	Do you eat fruits and vegetables every day?		
3	Do you try not to eat junk food?		
4	Do you drink only a little coffee or alcohol once in a while?		
5	Do you drink enough water?		
6	Do you go outside (work in a garden, go for a walk, ride a bike, etc.)?		
7	Do you do some exercise?		
8	Do you like what you study? Or do you like your job?		
9	Are you a nonsmoker?		
10	Do you relax every day?		
11	Do you sleep 7 to 9 hours a day?		
12	Do you visit your friends often?		
13	Are you close to your family?		
14	Do you have a positive mind?		
	Total	A	B

B Write the total number of **Yes** answers in A and **No** answers in B. Take B from A. Then find out how healthy you are on the score chart. For example: *(A = 7, B = 5) 7-5 = 2*

Scores:

11 – 14	A. You are very healthy! Keep it up!
8 – 10	B. You are doing pretty well. Well done.
5 – 7	C. You are doing okay. But you can do better.
0 – 4	D. Danger! Do something about your health!

Writing

Write a short essay about your lifestyle.

I'm not really healthy. I don't smoke, and I'm very close to my family. But I don't exercise, and I eat junk food too often . . .

Wrap-up

A Look at the pictures and complete the sentences with the correct words.

1.

She ______________ her head. (touch)
She has a ______________.

2.

She ______________ her nose with some tissues. (hold)
She has a ______________.

3.

He ______________. (cough)
He has a ______________.

B Complete the sentences by using imperatives.

1. ______________ too late. (not / stay up)
2. ______________ fruits and vegetables. (eat)
3. ______________ enough water. (drink)
4. ______________ too much coffee. (not / drink)
5. ______________ cigarettes. (not / smoke)

C Look at Jenny's schedule. Then answer the questions.

Jenny's Schedule	M	T	W	T	F	S	S
go to school	o	o	o	o	o		
watch movies						o	
do aerobics	o		o		o		
eat at a restaurant					o	o	

1. How many times a week does Jenny go to school?
2. How many times a week does Jenny watch movies?
3. How many times a week does Jenny do aerobics?
4. How many times a week does Jenny eat at a restaurant?

D What kind of lifestyle do you have? Do you think you are healthy? Why or why not?

Unit 10

Work and Jobs

Warm-up

Complete the job application checklist with your own information.

Job Application CHECKLIST

Myself

Name: ____________________

Phone: ____________________ Email: ____________________

I am over 18 years old. ☐ Yes ☐ No

I am interested in working in ☐ Sales ☐ Construction ☐ Service ☐ Education ☐ Management ☐ Manufacturing

I have a degree from ☐ high school ☐ university ☐ graduate school

Ability

I can use a computer. ☐ Yes ☐ No

[Answer only if you checked Yes above.]

I can use the following:

☐ word processing programs
☐ spreadsheets
☐ the Internet

I can drive. ☐ Yes ☐ No

[Answer only if you checked Yes above.]

☐ a motorcycle ☐ a car ☐ a truck

I can speak:

☐ English ☐ French ☐ Spanish
☐ Arabic ☐ Chinese ☐ Korean
☐ Japanese ☐ other: ____________________

Experience

I have work experience. ☐ Yes ☐ No

[Answer only if you checked Yes above.]

Department

☐ Sales ☐ Construction
☐ Service ☐ Education
☐ Management ☐ Manufacturing

Type

☐ internship
☐ part-time job
☐ full-time job

Place

☐ domestic
☐ international: ____________________

& More

I can work well with others. ☐ Yes ☐ No

I can work well by myself. ☐ Yes ☐ No

Can you cook?

Conversation

Listen and practice the conversation. 10-01

A Hey, can I use your laptop for a minute?
B Why?
A I'm looking for a part-time job.
B Really? What kind of job are you looking for?
A Anything is fine. I mean, I want a job near the campus. This restaurant is looking for a cook.
B Can you cook?
A No, I can't. But I can learn. I'm a fast learner.
B Well, good luck.

Grammar | *Can*

A Let's learn about permission and ability with *can*.

Permission	Ability
Can I **use** your phone? - Sure, you **can**. I don't have any pencils. - You **can use** mine. You **can't smoke** in this building.	Gerald **can cook** Italian food. They **cannot swim**. **Can** you **drive**? - Yes, I **can**. / No, I **can't**.
	* **be able to** I **can** solve this puzzle. = I **am able to** solve this puzzle.

B Fill the blanks with *can* or *can't*.

1. I ______________ surf, but I want to learn.
2. Gary is a great artist. He ______________ dance, sing, and even paint very well.
3. A ______________ I borrow your car? Mine is in the repair shop.
   B Sure. Here are the keys.
4. I am sorry, but I ______________ go to the party. I am sick.
5. Suzanna ______________ speak 4 languages: English, French, Spanish, and Italian.
6. A ______________ I use your computer?
   B I'm sorry, but my computer is broken.
7. A Why aren't you in bed?
   B I ______________ sleep.
8. A I don't have any money.
   B I ______________ lend you some.

Listening

A Listen to the phone conversation and answer the questions. 10-02

1. What do Benjamin and his friend want to do this weekend?
   a. go skiing
   b. go hiking
   c. go swimming
2. Which is true about Benjamin?
   a. He teaches people how to ski.
   b. He doesn't like to ski much.
   c. He can't ski well. He falls down all the time.

B Listen to the phone conversation. Then check which activities Benjamin can do.

☐ cook ☐ play computer games ☐ type ☐ ride a bike ☐ walk to work

How well can you do it?

A Let's learn about *a little*, *very well*, and *can't ~ at all*.

B Look at the pictures and complete the sentences with the correct words.

1.

The girl ______________ sing ______________.

2.

The boy ______________ ride a bike ______________.

3.

The cheetah ______________ run ______________.

C Say 3 things you can do well and 3 things you can't do at all.

I can cook very well. I can't play the piano at all . . .

Is doing an internship good or bad?

Reading

Read about the two students' opinions about internships. 10-03

Doing an internship at a big company is a great opportunity. First, interns can learn new things at the company. Second, they can meet lots of people in the industry. Companies can help interns find jobs when they graduate. Finally, interns can make their résumés stronger because of their internship experience. Companies can even give their interns jobs after the internships are finished. Who knows?

Justin

Kenji

In my opinion, internships are a waste of time. First, companies don't let interns do anything interesting. Interns just get some documents from this person and take them to that person. It's really boring. Sometimes they make coffee for people. Second, companies love interns because they don't always pay interns. Last, when the internships finish, companies don't always hire their interns because they don't have enough money. So interns do all that work for nothing.

Comprehension Check Complete the summaries of Justin's and Kenji's opinions.

1. Justin: Internships are good!

a. Interns can learn new things.

b. ______________________________

c. ______________________________

VS

2. Kenji: Internships are a waste of time!

a. Interns can't do anything interesting. Their jobs are boring.

b. ______________________________

c. ______________________________

Listening

Listen to the phone conversation and choose True or False. 10-04

1. Lily is doing an internship. [True / False]
2. Lily likes it because she is making money. [True / False]
3. Erin is going for an interview. [True / False]
4. Erin doesn't like boring work. [True / False]
5. Erin can't make any money by working for the Cameron Insurance Company. [True / False]

Looking for a Job

Reading

A Read the job ads. 10-05

Looking for CLEANERS $9/hour

Restroom cleaners wanted at Funland Amusement Park. You can choose to work mornings or evenings. We only want hard workers to apply. No experience necessary. Call Simon at 816-3949.

Fruit Pickers Wanted

Fruit pickers wanted at Smith & Sons Farm. Are you a hard worker? Can you be your own boss and work alone? If you can, we can pay you $26 for each bin you fill. You can make good money here. If you are interested, please call Margaret Smith at 0489-564-4390.

CONSTRUCTION WORKERS NEEDED $20/hour

You have to be able to lift over 50 kilograms. This job requires hard labor with lots of lifting and pulling. Some experience preferred. Call Dan at 409-9812.

B Look at the pictures and answer the questions.

1. Which job above best matches his ability?
2. How much can he make per hour from that job?

3. Which job above best matches her schedule?
4. Who does she need to call?

5. Which job above best matches his ability?
6. What number does he need to call?

Writing

Write a short essay about your ideal job. Think about what you can do and what kind of work you want to do.

A fitness trainer at a gym is my ideal job. I am majoring in physical education. I am active and very friendly. I want to help others to have healthy lives.

I want a job.

Listening

A Listen to the conversation and answer the questions. 10-06

1. What does the woman want the man to look at?
   a. her email b. her résumé c. her application form
2. For what position is the woman applying?
   a. salesperson b. assistant manager c. accounting assistant
3. What is the woman studying?
   a. business b. nursing c. French
4. How many hours does the woman want to work?
   a. 16 hours a day b. 16 hours a week c. 16 hours a month

B Listen to the talk. Then choose the correct information about the woman.

Application Form

Name **1.** (Jessica / Jane) Lynn Kelly
Education Cardenas College (4th year)
2. Majoring in (science / science technology)

Strengths **3.** (Hardworking / Happy), diligent, and motivated
Hobbies **4.** (Reading books / Watching movies)
Volunteer Work Reading books at a **5.** (school / hospital)

TIPS & TIPS Years in College or University

first year	second year	third year	fourth year
freshman	sophomore	junior	senior

He is in his third year at a law school.
I am a sophomore at State University.

Pair Work

Imagine you are at a job interview and your partner is the interviewer. Introduce yourself. Take turns.

Good morning. My name is Addison Carlton. I am a junior at Central Modern Art College. I am majoring in art history . . .

Conversation

Listen and practice the conversation. 10-07

A So tell me why you want to work in our Sales Department?

B I think I can be a good salesperson. I am confident, active, and very friendly.

A I see . . . We do a lot of work in China. Can you speak Chinese?

B Yes, I can.

A Good. Can you work on holidays and weekends?

B Of course. That's not a problem.

A Great. One more thing. Can you drive a car? We need our salespeople to visit our clients.

B No, but I am able to learn quickly.

Vocabulary | Parts of a Company

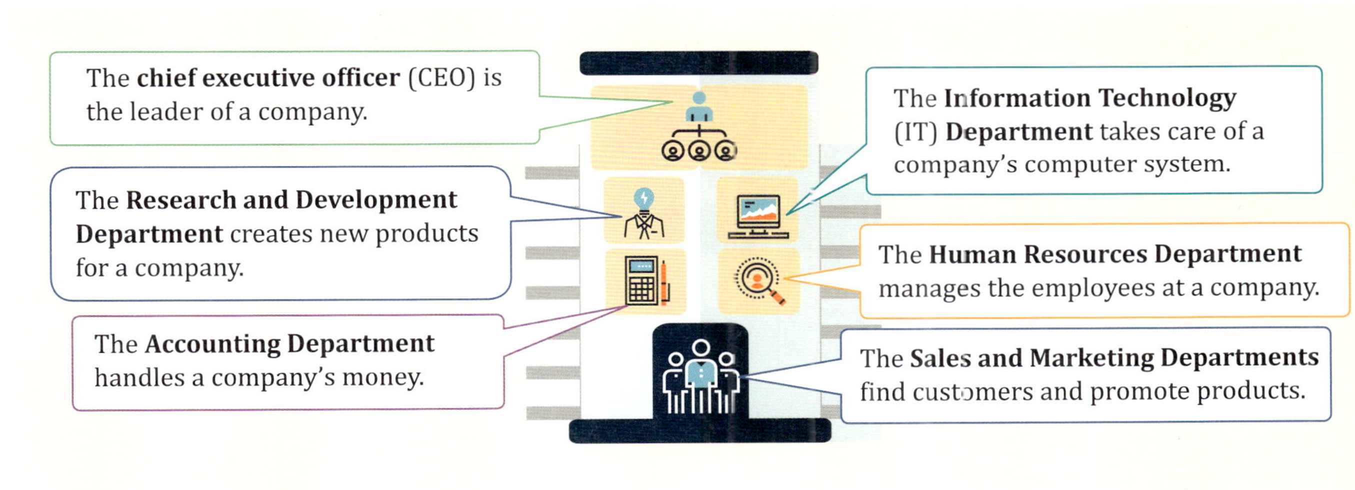

Speaking

Read the answers. Unscramble the sentences to make correct questions. Then practice the conversations.

Q1: (strengths / are / what / your) ______________________________?

A1: *I always try to do my best with everything I do.*

Q2: (about / your / education / can / you / me / tell) ______________________________?

A2: *I am a senior at Campus University. I am majoring in architecture. / I have a degree from a university.*

Q3: (and / weekends / holidays / can / work / you / on) ______________________________?

A3: *Sure, I can.*

Q4: (hobbies / what / are / your) ______________________________?

A4: *I like watching movies and taking walks.*

Q5: (when / you / start / can) ______________________________?

A5: *I can start next Monday.*

Opportunities Abroad

Reading

A Read the online newsletter *Student Abroad Monthly*. 10-08

Student Abroad Monthly

A Letter from a Student

Greetings from Down Under

Hi, everyone. This is Jeremy.

It's another great day in Australia.

This is my second week at a new vineyard. The good news is I can now pick grapes without cutting my fingers! Of course, work is still difficult. I wake up around 5 a.m. every day. Sometimes I take breaks and work for 7~8 hours. Sometimes I work more than 9 hours a day. Days off? Only when it rains! But it's okay because if you work hard here, you can make good money. Imagine what you can do with the money you save!

Click HERE to read more.

Want overseas opportunities?

Study Abroad -Scotland-

We invite business majors to Edinburgh.

Click HERE to learn more.

Volunteers Needed *Dominican Republic*

We are looking for healthy and strong volunteers.

Click HERE to learn more.

Internship Opportunity!

The Mexico Fashion Design Center is looking for smart, hardworking students!

Click HERE to learn more.

Comprehension Check Answer the questions about the online newsletter.

1. What is Jeremy doing in Australia?
2. What time does Jeremy usually wake up?
3. When can Jeremy have a day off?
4. What does Jeremy think of working hard? Why does he think that way?
5. How many overseas opportunities does the newsletter show?
6. Which overseas opportunity gives students a chance to work with fashion designers?

B Read the full ad about the volunteer program in the Dominican Republic. Then answer the questions.

Volunteers Needed
Dominican Republic

Because of the recent flooding in the Dominican Republic, many families cannot find clean drinking water or good housing. We are looking for healthy and strong volunteers. Come and help us rebuild the country. Can you help dig wells for fresh drinking water? Can you help build houses? If the answers are yes, please contact Shauna at savedr@mail.net.

1. What kinds of volunteers are they looking for?
2. What can volunteers do to help the Dominican Republic?
3. Can you volunteer for this program?

Listening

A Listen to the three phone conversations. Then write the names Julia, Dan, and Lucy in the correct places.

10-09

1.

England

2.

Myanmar

3.

Portugal

B Listen again and choose the correct words.

1. Julia can work with (fashion designers / architects).
2. Julia (can / cannot) go home for summer vacation.
3. Dan's friend (can / can't) work for free.
4. Lucy wants to (travel / work) around Europe.
5. Lucy's school in England has a (two-week / three-week) break.

Speaking

Imagine that you can study or do an internship abroad. What do you want to do, and where do you want to go? Why?

I want to do an internship as a chef. I think I want to go to Italy. I want to learn about Italian food.

Wrap-up

A Look at the table. Then write sentences about what Brook can and cannot do.

1. *Brook can* ________________
2. ________________
3. ________________
4. ________________
5. ________________

play sports	O
use a computer	X
cook	O
speak French	O
dance	X

B Read the people's opinions about internships. Then put the names in the correct places.

"Interns work hard, but they don't always make money for their work."
Cory, USA

"Internships can help students find jobs after they graduate."
Ada, Germany

"Interns can get a lot of work experience during an internship."
Eunmi, South Korea

"Many interns do boring work like making copies or coffee."
Rana, Egypt

Doing an internship is a good idea.	Internships are a waste of time.
,	,

C Read about Halim. Then fill out the application form for him.

Application Form

Position Applied: Junior Researcher
Name: 1. ____________
Education: 2. ____________ University
Year / Major: 4th year / 3. ____________
Strengths: problem-solver
& 4. ____________
Hobbies: 5. ____________ & swimming

My name is Halim. I live in Jakarta, Indonesia. I am a senior at Jakarta State University. My major is biology. I am a problem-solver. I can see problems differently and understand them better. I am a good listener, too. I like playing soccer with my friends in my free time. I also like swimming.

D Imagine that you want to volunteer for a month. What do you want to do? Where do you want to go?

Unit 11 Experience

Warm-up

Five people describe important events in their lives. Put the names in the correct places.

- A.J.: "I went to Paris last year."
- Hana: "Darren and I graduated from high school in 2015."
- Marilyn: "I started working at an animal clinic in 2010."
- Danny: "My sister got married 3 years ago."
- Li Wei: "I was born in 1998."

1. ________

2. ________

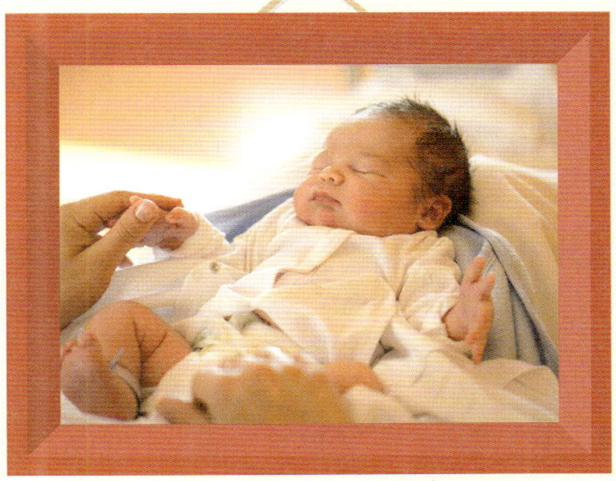

3. ________

4. ________

5. ________

You were so cute.

Conversation

Listen and practice the conversation. 11-01

A Oh, is that you, Helen?
B Of course it is. You know I'm an only child.
A You were so cute. Was it a special day?
B I think it was my 5th birthday. The picture has the date on it. Let's see . . . I was right. It was March 9th, 1996.
A So, you were born on March 9th.
B Yes, I was.
A No way! I was born on March 9th, too!

TIPS & TIPS How to Say Years

1900 = nineteen hundred	2000 = two thousand
1905 = nineteen oh five	2002 = two thousand (and) two
1995 = nineteen ninety-five	2010 = two thousand (and) ten OR twenty-ten

Q. Say the years.
1803 / 2014 / 1988 / the year you were born

Grammar | Past Simple Tense: *Be*

A Let's learn about the past simple forms of *be*.

am → **was** are → **were** is → **was**	I **was** cute. Some children **were** on the beach. Gregory **was** happy. We **were** friends.	I **wasn't** tall. They **were** not here. **Was** Cindy in English class yesterday? Where **were** your parents?

B Complete the sentences with the correct forms of *be*.

1. I ______________ a high school student in 1999.
2. A ______________ you in science class?
   B No, I ______________.
3. Most of the students ______________ late for class. (not)

C Rewrite the sentences in the past simple tense.

1. It is sunny today. → ________________________________ yesterday.
2. Jack and Jill are 10 years old this year. → ________________________________ last year.
3. I am tired. → ________________________________ last night.
4. You are upset. → ________________________________ one hour ago.

Listening

A Listen to the conversation and choose the correct words. 11-02

1. The speakers moved into a (new / old) place.
2. The speakers' new place is big and (dark / bright).
3. The speakers' old place was old and (cheap / smelly).
4. The speakers' old neighbors weren't (nice / rude).
5. The speakers are (happy / unhappy) about their new place.

B Listen again and check the words you hear.

☐ old	☐ important	☐ difficult	☐ nice	☐ high
☐ calm	☐ cheap	☐ smelly	☐ early	☐ disgusting

Vocabulary | Adjectives for Feelings and Emotions

A Let's learn more adjectives.

happy satisfied confident proud glad	surprised confused amazed excited	bad bored stressed tired	sad lonely hurt depressed	angry upset mad frustrated disgusted

B Look at the pictures. Then describe the people's feelings with adjectives.

1. 
2. 
3. 
4. 

C Talk about your feelings with adjectives.

I was bored yesterday, but I am happy today.

Did you do anything fun?

Conversation

Listen and practice the conversation. 11-03

A Hey, Tom, how was your vacation? Did you do anything fun?
B Of course. I visited my friend in Los Angeles.
A Los Angeles? Wow. What did you do?
B I walked on the Santa Monica beach every day. I played volleyball there. It was amazing.
A Did you go to Universal Studios?
B No. I didn't have time.
A That's too bad.
B Maybe next time. How was your vacation, Bea?
A Mine was amazing, too. I stayed at home and watched TV.

Grammar | Past Simple Tense: Regular Verbs

A Let's learn about the past simple forms of regular verbs.

Spelling: stay → **stayed** like → **liked**	study → **studied** stop → **stopped**
I **opened** the door. Jerry **watched** a movie last night.	Some students **played** badminton. We **used** the airport shuttle last time.
Did you **live** in Japan last year? **Did** Jonas **call** Mark? When **did** the rain **stop**? How **did** Mimi **open** this bottle?	Mr. Sanchez **didn't remember** the directions. You **didn't believe** me. The reporters **didn't ask** many questions. June **didn't walk** home last night.

B Complete the sentences with the correct forms of the verbs.

1. The Robinsons ______________ at a nice hotel last weekend. (stay)
2. John ______________ at the club all night. (dance)
3. The rain finally ______________ an hour ago. (stop)
4. When ______________ you ______________ at school? (arrive)

C Rewrite the sentences in the past simple tense.

1. I visit my grandparents every fall. → ______________________________ last fall.
2. Does Carrie work at a department store? → ______________________________ last year?
3. The photographers don't follow the wolves. → ______________________________ two days ago.
4. We check our email every night. → ______________________________ last night.

Listening

A Listen to the phone message. Then choose True or False. 11-04

1. The speaker did not enjoy his trip. [True / False]
2. The speaker missed the plane. [True / False]
3. The speaker was on an old and dirty plane. [True / False]
4. The speaker lost his camera. [True / False]

B Listen to the phone conversation. Then complete the report w th the correct words or numbers.

Lost & Found Report		
Hilltop Hotel 987-254-3345 / cshilltop@greathotel.com		
Date: June 1st	☐ Lost	☑ Found
Guest Information Name: Harrison Simon Contact no.: 987-665-5555 Room no. **1.** ____________ / May 28th (**2.** ____________ nights)		
Description of item(s): a silver **3.** ____________ with a **4.** ____________ strap		

Pair Work

Play the board game with your partner.

Rules

1. Put a marker on START. Any small items can be markers.
2. Flip a coin. **Heads: move one space. Tails: move two spaces.**
3. Make a sentence or question in the past simple tense.
   For example: *not / clean / room / last week → I didn't clean my room last week.*
4. When you make a question, your partner answers.

START ➡	call / a friend / last night	not / check / my email / this morning	Start Over	watch / a movie / last weekend / ?
				Free Space
Skip a Turn	not / bake / cookies	enjoy / dancing	Move 2 Spaces Forward	when / arrive / school / ?
what song / like the most / ?				
not / pick / the flower	Move 2 Spaces Back	collect / stamps / a long time ago / ?	hate / vegetables	FINISH

Q. Did you win the game? Did you enjoy it?

What happened yesterday?

Vocabulary | Everyday Activities

Put the words and phrases in the correct places.

see someone	sleep	make food	do the laundry
do the dishes	spend time online	take a shower	call a friend

1. 

2. 

3. 

4. 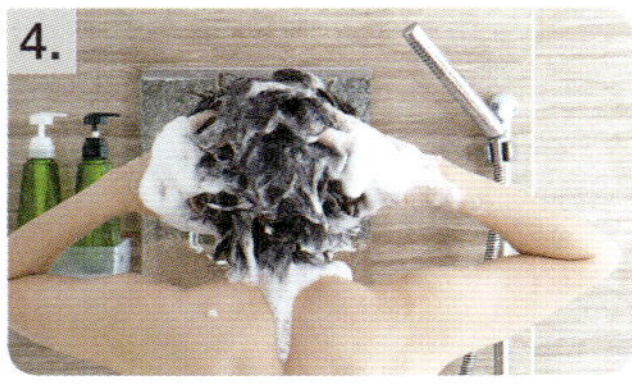

5. 

6. 

7. 

8. 

Q. How often do you do these activities above?

Conversation

Listen and practice the conversation. 11-05

A Hello?
B Hey, Mom. Can you see me?
A Yes, I can! What happened yesterday? We called you, but you didn't answer.
B Well, it got really cold in Chicago, so I got sick.
A Oh, no! Did you see a doctor?
B No, I didn't. My roommate made me some chicken soup. I took a hot shower. Then I slept all day.
A Do you feel better now?
B Yes, I do. I felt much better when I woke up. I went to the movies with my roommate. I even did the laundry.
A Oh, that's good.

Pair Work

What did you do yesterday and last weekend? Talk with your partner.

A What did you do yesterday?
B I went to a movie. How about you?
A I made dinner for my family.

A What did you do last weekend?
B I stayed at home and watched TV. How about you?
A I helped my mom clean the house.

Grammar | Past Simple Tense: Irregular Verbs

A Let's learn more about the past simple forms of irregular verbs.

buy → **bought**	drink → **drank**	have → **had**	read → **read**	take → **took**
come → **came**	eat → **ate**	make → **made**	say → **said**	teach → **taught**
do → **did**	go → **went**	put → **put**	see → **saw**	write → **wrote**

I **did** my laundry last night. Holly **made** dinner for her sister.	Mr. Scott **taught** math last year. Many people **bought** this car.
Did your parents **come** home last weekend? What did you **say**?	The man **didn't read** any newspapers. Ivy **didn't take** this class last semester.

You can find a list of more irregular verbs on page 148.

B Complete the sentences with the correct forms of the verbs.

1. The Millers ______________ some bread and eggs for breakfast. (have)
2. ______________ you ______________ your homework? (do)
3. He ______________ some sun cream on his face one hour ago. (put)

C Rewrite the sentences in the past simple tense.

1. My mom drinks a cup of coffee every morning. → __________________________________ yesterday morning.
2. The farmer goes to bed early. → __________________________________ last night.
3. Veronica reads two books a month. → __________________________________ last month.

Listening

A Listen and complete the conversation. 11-06

A So?

B Carlos ______________ me to a nice ______________ near the town hall. He ______________ some steaks and ______________ for us.

A Wine?

B Yes. We ate and drank. We had a wonderful time. Suddenly, he held my hand and ______________.

A Oh, my goodness. You're kidding!

B Then he ______________, "Maria, my darling, please pay for dinner. I ______________ to bring my ______________."

A What?

B I ______________ more than $300 on dinner last night.

B Listen again and answer the questions.

1. Where did Carlos and Maria go last night?
2. What did Carlos and Maria drink?
3. What did Carlos forget to bring?

Learning Vacation Reviews

Reading

Read three online reviews. 11-07

Winemaking in France *by Allen*

I arrived at the vineyard and met Pierre. Over the next three weeks, he taught me about winemaking. I tasted many different types of wine, too. It was hard work. Pierre sometimes yelled at me, but he was a good teacher. I learned so much about wine. At the end, I took 5 bottles home with me. I love them!

Learning to Fly-Fish in Montana *by Francis*

I met Jim at the Montana airport. He brought me to a guesthouse near the river. That day, he started teaching me how to fly-fish. I practiced all day long. The next day, I was able to do it well! It was amazing. The area was beautiful, and the fish were really big. I caught a fish on my first day. We cooked it for dinner that night. It was one of the best days of my life!

Want to Learn How to Dive? Think Again! *by Alexandra*

A driver picked me up at the airport. Then he took me to the hotel. I wanted to take scuba diving lessons that same day, but no one came to the hotel. I emailed the company many times. I waited for a reply, but no one replied. Two days later, the company sent a man. His name was Miguel. He didn't speak any English. So I wasn't able to learn much. I was really angry.

Comprehension Check Answer the questions about the vacation reviews.

1. Where did Allen go on vacation?
2. Who taught Allen how to make wine?
3. When did Francis learn to fly-fish?
4. What did Alexandra want to learn on vacation?
5. Why did Alexandra have a bad time on her vacation?

Speaking

When was the last time you learned something new? Describe your experience.

My sister and I took a cooking class last month. We learned how to bake cakes and cookies. The teacher was very friendly.

Listening

A Listen to two people talk about their trips. How was the weather? Check the correct pictures. 11-08

1. Name: Cynthia Place: Morocco

a.  ☐

b.  ☐

2. Name: Ross Place: London

a.  ☐

b.  ☐

B Listen again and choose True or False.

1. Cynthia went to Morocco alone. [True / False]
2. Cynthia went to a night market. [True / False]
3. Cynthia wants to give it five stars. [True / False]
4. Ross stayed in London for a month. [True / False]
5. Ross didn't like London because it was too expensive. [True / False]
6. Ross liked London Bridge. [True / False]

Writing

Write a review about your recent vacation. How many stars out of 5 do you want to give it? Color the star(s).

Title:

☆☆☆☆☆

Questions to think about:

- Where did you go?
- Who did you go with?
- How long did you stay?
- How was the weather?
- What did you do there?
- Did you have a good time? Why or why not?
- How many stars out of 5 do you want to give it?

Wrap-up

A Answer the questions with years.

1. In what year was your mother born?
2. In what year did you meet your best friend?
3. In what year did you get your first cell phone?
4. In what year were you 10 years old?

B Complete the sentences with the correct forms of *be*.

1. She ______________ a good student when she was young.
2. You ______________ the goalkeeper on the team. (not)
3. I ______________ born in a small town. (not)
4. ______________ Jerry and Elizabeth married in a big church?

C Complete the conversation with the correct forms of the verbs.

1. A ______________ you ______________ the baseball game last night? (see)
   B No, I didn't. I ______________ late. (work)
2. A Hey, Mom. ______________ you ______________ to the doctor's office yesterday? (go)
   B Yes, I ______________. (do) He ______________ me some medicine for the flu. (give)
   A ______________ you ______________ it? (take)
   B Yes, I ______________ it before you called. (take)
3. A ______________ you ______________ the food? (enjoy)
   B Yes, I did. I ______________ a lot. (eat)
   A Would you like some dessert?
   B No, thanks.

D Be a food critic and give a rating to a restaurant you went to recently. Then write about it.

Name	
Food	☆ ☆ ☆ ☆ ☆
Price	☆ ☆ ☆ ☆ ☆
Service	☆ ☆ ☆ ☆ ☆
Overall	☆ ☆ ☆ ☆ ☆

Unit
12 Plans

Warm-up

Look at Rob's calendar. Then answer the questions.

June

Sun.	Mon.	Tue.	Wed.	Thur.	Fri.	Sat.
1	2 Sales Meeting	3	4 Business Trip	5 Business Trip	6 Business Trip	7 Tennis Lessons
8	9 Sales Meeting	10	11 Lunch with Brian	12	13	14 Fishing Trip
15 Fishing Trip	16 Day Off	17 Mom's Birthday Party	18	19	20	21 Tennis Lessons
22 Ken's & Karen's Wedding	23 Sales Meeting	24	25	26 Dinner With Flora	27	28 Tennis Lessons
29	30 Sales Meeting					

1. On which day is Rob going to have a sales meeting?
2. What is going to happen on the 22nd of June?
3. For how long is Rob going to go on a business trip?
4. When is Rob going to go fishing?
5. How many times is Rob going to have tennis lessons in June?

Weekend Plans

Conversation

Listen and practice the conversation. 12-01

A Are you going to do anything special this weekend, Aaron?
B I'm going to go to the ballet with my wife.
A No way! I thought you were a sports fan!
B Well, I don't really like the ballet, but my wife loves it.
A I'm in a similar situation. I don't like sports, but my husband is a big sports fan. He is going to take me to a basketball game.
B I will trade weekends with you. I will go to the basketball game with your husband.
A And I will go to the ballet with your wife. Perfect!

Grammar | *Be going to* and *Will*

A Let's learn about *be going to* and *will*.

Be going to *for something you planned before*	
I **am going to see** a **movie** tomorrow. It **is going to rain** this afternoon. We **are going to go** hiking this weekend.	I'**m not going to go** out tonight. Kate **isn't going to have** a meeting tomorrow. Sue and Marco **aren't going to come** to the party next Friday.
Is the school **going to close** next Monday?	**What are** you **going to do** tonight?

Will *for something you just decided to do*	
I'll take a break in an hour. The staff members **will work** late tonight. **What** drink **will** you **have**, sir? - I **will have** an espresso.	**Will** you **have** some coffee? **What time will** Grace **call** Megan? How about this blouse, ma'am? - It's perfect. I'**ll take** it.

B Complete the sentences by using *be going to* or *will*.

1. She ______________________ her grandmother this weekend. (visit)
2. I ______________________ her on Saturday. (call)
3. We ______________________ a taxi. (take) We ______________________ late. (not / be)
4. They ______________________ a test tomorrow. (not / take)
5. A Are you ready to order, sir?
   B Yes. I ______________________ the steak and potatoes. (have)
6. I ______________________ from high school next month. (graduate)
7. Where ______________________ her friend? (meet)
8. ______________________ soccer on Tuesday? (play)

Listening

A Listen to the conversation and answer the questions. 12-02

1. What is the first thing Tommy is going to do this weekend? Choose the correct picture.

2. What is the last thing Suzy is going to do this weekend? Choose the correct picture.

a. 

b. 

c. 

d. 

B Listen again and choose the correct words.

1. On Saturday morning, Tommy is going to take his kids to ______________.
   a. an amusement park　　b. the library　　c. the movies

2. On Saturday, Tommy's family is going to visit his wife's ______________.
   a. grandparents　　b. aunt and uncle　　c. parents

3. On Saturday, Suzy is going to ______________.
   a. meet a friend　　b. see a movie　　c. stay home

4. On Sunday, Suzy is going to ______________.
   a. go shopping for groceries　　b. wash her car　　c. sleep in

Speaking

A Look at Ian's Saturday list. Then say what he is going to do and what he is not going to do this Saturday.

Do these!
Send Mom birthday flowers
Watch the DVD & return it to Hanson
Wash the bedsheets and curtains

Don't do these!
Drink too much beer
Spend too much time online
Stay up too late on Saturday night

He is going to call his mom. He is not going to go to the gym . . .

B Say three things that you are going to do this weekend.

I am going to have brunch with my best friend on Saturday morning . . .

Over the Holidays

Conversation

Listen and practice the conversation. 12-03

A Are you going to go anywhere over the Christmas holiday?

B I'm going to visit my family in Florida. My sister and I are going to spend a lot of time at the beach.

A Sounds great! When are you going to leave?

B I'm going to leave tomorrow.

A So soon? When are you going to come back?

B On December 31st.

A Oh, good timing. You will come to my New Year's Eve party, won't you?

Vocabulary | Things to Do over the Holidays

party

concert

beach

movie theater

rafting

hiking

snowboarding

snorkeling

Many people are going to go to Christmas **parties**.

Chelsea is going to go to the **movie theater** on Thanksgiving Day.

My friends and I are going to go **rafting** during our summer vacation.

Perry's family is going to go **hiking** this holiday.

Q. What other activities do you do on holidays?

Class Activity

Play charades with your classmates.

Rules

1. Divide the class into two groups: A and B.
2. One person from Group A acts out a holiday activity in front of Group B.
3. Group B has to guess by saying: *You are going to go surfing.*
4. The correct answer gets one point. The group with more points wins.

Expressions for the Future

Let's learn some expressions for the future.

soon	The flight is going to take off **soon**.
in an hour	I'm going to leave **in an hour**.
later this morning/afternoon/evening	The Adams are going to see a movie **later this evening**.
tomorrow	It's not going to be sunny **tomorrow**.
the day after tomorrow	Are you going to come to school **the day after tomorrow**?
next week/month/year	Ellie is going to study abroad **next year**.
in the future	What are you going to do **in the future**?

Pair Work

Practice the conversations with your partner.

A What are you going to do in two hours?
B I am going to go to the library.

A What are you going to do tomorrow?
B I am going to watch a movie with a friend.

Listening

A Listen to the conversation and choose True or False. 12-04

1. Alex has a lot of work to do over the holidays. [True / False]
2. Alex's family is going to go skiing over the holidays. [True / False]
3. Brown Bear Mountain is a great ski resort. [True / False]

B Listen to the second part of the conversation. Then answer the questions.

1. What day is Ben's family going to leave?
   a. Friday   b. Saturday   c. Sunday
2. How are they going to get there?
   a. on foot   b. by train   c. by car
3. What time are they going to leave?
   a. 6 a.m.   b. 7 a.m.   c. 8 a.m.
4. What is Alex going to do over the holiday?
   a. He is going to work at home.   b. He is going to go skiing   c. He is going to see his boss.

Writing

Write a short essay about your holiday plans.

Questions to think about:
- Where are you going to go?
- Who are you going to go with?
- How long are you going to stay?
- What are you going to do there?

Inviting and Accepting/Declining an Invitation

Conversation 1

Listen and practice the conversation. 12-05

A Hello.
B Ramos, it's Nick.
A Hey, Nick. What's up?
B Are you free on Sunday?
A Yeah. I am just going to stay home and watch TV this weekend.
B Great. I have an extra ticket for the baseball game on Sunday. Would you like to come?
A A baseball game? Sure. I'd love to.

Pair Work

Practice the conversation with your partner.

A Would you like to get some coffee?
B Sure. That sounds good.

A Would like to come to my birthday party?
B I'd love to.

Conversation 2

Listen and practice the conversation. 12-06

A Good work today.
B Ah, thanks. You, too.
A Do you have any plans for tonight?
B Actually, I do. I'm going to go to the movies. Would you like to come?
A I'd love to, but I can't. I am going to have dinner with my parents.
B Oh, okay. Maybe next time.

Pair Work

Practice the conversation with your partner. Give excuses. You can use reasons in the box below or your own ideas.

A Would you like to go shopping tonight?
B I'd love to, but I can't. I am going to visit my parents.

A Would you like to hang out this weekend?
B I am afraid I can't. I am going to go away for the weekend.

Possible Reasons:	go away for the weekend	go to the movies
	visit friends or family members	study for an exam

Listening

A Listen to the conversation and answer the questions. 12-07

1. What are the speakers talking about?
   a. their party   b. their vacations   c. their wedding
2. Who is going to come to the speakers' house?
   a. Lola   b. Santiago   c. Minju

B Listen again and choose the correct answers.

1. When is the event?
   a. Friday   b. Saturday   c. Sunday
2. Why are Chris and Carl not going to come to the event?
   a. because they are sick
   b. because they don't like the speakers
   c. because they don't know about the event

Class Activity | Party Invitation

A Make groups of three. Each group chooses one party in the table. Then plan the party.

	Birthday / Graduation / Housewarming / Christmas Party
Date & Time	
Place	
Food & Drink	
Decorations & Music	

B Write an invitation notice. Then each group shows the invitation and invites the class to the party.

Our group is going to have a birthday party for Jenny. It is going to be on the 29th of June at 7 p.m. . . . Would you like to come?

C One student draws the table below on a piece of paper and lists all the parties. Then he or she passes the paper around the class. Everyone accepts invitations by writing his or her name on the piece of paper or declines them by writing his or her name with an excuse.

Party Name	Who would like to come	Who can't come / Why
Sandra's Birthday	*Maxim Julia Nick*	*Gregory / going to be away*

Q. How many parties are you going to go to?
How many people are going to come to your group's party?

Unusual Tours

Reading

Read about three unusual places for a trip. 12-08

Something a Little Different

Every year, millions of people travel to famous cities or beautiful islands. But what do you do if you want something different? Why don't you try one of these unusual trips?

A Creepy Hollywood Tour

Visit Los Angeles and go on the Creepy Hollywood Bus Tour. Do you like ghost stories? Then it's perfect for you. On this tour, you are going to visit Mann's Chinese Theater. Do you know about the ghost there? An actor died there in the 1920s, but he never left the theater! You are also going to learn about the Black Dahlia murder. This is an unsolved crime from the 1940s. L.A. is warm, but bring a jacket because there are going to be lots of chills.

A Hobbit Village Tour

Do you love *The Lord of the Rings* movies? Visit New Zealand, and you can see Hobbiton. It's the hobbit village from the movies. On the tour, your group is going to visit the homes of your favorite characters. You are even going to go inside a hobbit's home, too. Book your tour NOW because it is very popular.

A Trip to Space

Did you want to be an astronaut when you were young? It is not too late. Space X can help you. This company sells private flights to space for one million dollars. It is a lot of money, but as a passenger on a Space X spacecraft, you are going to float in zero gravity. You are going to look at the Earth from outer space. And you are going to eat real astronaut food. Yes, it is expensive, but it is going to make your dreams come true.

Comprehension Check Answer the questions about the unusual tours.

1. Which tour is in the city of Los Angeles?
2. What is the name of the hobbit village in New Zealand?
3. Why do people want to book their hobbit village tour early?
4. How much does it cost to go to space on a Space X spacecraft?
5. What are people going to do as passengers on a Space X flight?

Listening

A Listen to the conversation and choose the correct words. 12-09

1. The man is going to go to New York City next (week / month).
2. The man is going to go there for (fun / business).
3. The man wants to visit (Chinatown / Dumbo).
4. The man is going to cross the Brooklyn Bridge (on foot / by subway).

B Listen to the talk about a half-day tour in New York City. Then number the pictures in the correct order.

☐ We are going to take the ferry to Liberty Island.

☐ We are going to have free time on Ellis Island.

☐ We are going to go to the museum in the Statue of Liberty.

☐ We are going to go up to the observation deck.

Writing

Imagine you are going to go on a trip for 3 days. Where are you going to go? What are you going to do? Plan the trip. Then write about it.

3-Day Trip to ______________

Day 1 What: ______________

Day 2 What: ______________

Day 3 What: ______________

I am going to go to Bangkok for 3 days. On the first day, I am going to visit temples . . .

Wrap-up

A Complete the sentences by using *be going to* or *will*.

1. I have a lot of homework. I ______________ out tonight. (not / go)
2. Kelly and Jennifer ______________ camping this weekend. (go)
3. ______________ Hamin ______________ his mother this weekend? (call)
4. A ______________ you ______________ the call? (take) It's Mr. Moore.
   B No, I am busy. I ______________ him back. (call)
5. A What ______________ your parents ______________ this summer? (do)
   B ______________ around Europe. (travel)

B Match the questions to the correct answers.

1. How are we going to get there?
2. When are you going to arrive?
3. What are you going to do after graduation?
4. I'm not going to be able to meet you today. How about tomorrow?

a. I am only a freshman. I don't know what I'm going to do in the future.
b. I am going to be there soon.
c. Saturday? Sure. The day after tomorrow is good, too.
d. We are going to take a taxi.

C Invite your partner to do something in the future.

Would you like to come to . . .

D Imagine you are going to show a friend around your city this weekend. Where are you going to take him or her? What are you going to do? Plan the trip. Then write about it.

Weekend Plans in ______________		
	Places to Visit	Things to Do
Saturday		
Sunday		

Answer Key

Unit 1 Introducing Myself

My name is Maria Smith.

Grammar p. 13

B

1. His 2. My 3. Their
4. Our 5. Her 6. Its
7. Their

I am from Mexico.

Listening p. 15

Script

1. Hello. My name is Luong. I'm Vietnamese. I'm from Vietnam.
2. Hi. I'm Wendy. I'm from England. I'm English.
3. What's up? I'm Pedro. I'm Mexican. I'm from Mexico.

A

1. Vietnam 2. England 3. Mexico

Script

1. Hello. My name is Anna Papadopoulos. I'm a student. I'm from Athens. I'm Greek. My country has many museums.
2. Good afternoon. I'm Miguel Alvarez. I'm a driver. I'm from South America. I'm Argentinian. Many famous soccer players are Argentinian, too.
3. Hi. My name is Heidi Glaser. I'm a doctor. I'm from Bern. I'm Swiss. I love the Swiss Alps.
4. Good morning. I am Kumar Apu. I am an engineer. I'm Indian. My home is in Bangalore. I am here with my family.
5. What's up? My name's Jason Walters. I'm an English teacher. I'm from Los Angeles, California. So I'm American. L.A. is beautiful. I love the weather there.

B

1. b 2. c 3. a
4. a 5. a

What's your phone number?

Listening p. 17

Script

1. Hello. I'm Lisa. Please call me back. My phone number is 478-7898.
2. Hello. I'm Justin Maunder. Please send me an email. My email address is j_maunder@privatemail.com.
3. Hello, Ms. Hamels. This is Jorge Maitan. Please call me back. My telephone number is 925-6192.
4. Hi, Mr. Gonzales. Send an email to Kate. Her email address is kate_85@etz.edu.

1. a 2. a 3. b
4. a

She's a chef.

Reading p. 18

Comprehension Check

1. Rome, Italian 2. American, Chicago
3. Beijing, tour guide 4. Pedro, Chilean

Vocabulary p. 18

A

doctor, 3 police officer, 1
pilot, 2 actor/actress, 6
singer, 5 soccer player, 4

Wrap-up p. 20

B

France	French	China	Chinese
Germany	German	Australia	Australian
Italy	Italian	Vietnam	Vietnamese
United States	American	Malaysia	Malaysian
Mexico	Mexican	Saudi Arabia	Saudi Arabian

Unit 2 My Family and Friends

Warm-up p. 21

A

1. grandmother 2. son 3. parents
4. wife

Do you have a sister?

Grammar p. 23

B

1. Do you have a sister
2. How old is he
3. Does she have a daughter
4. How old are they

They are both kind!

Reading p. 24

Karen's grandfather: John Lewis , 72, Australian, tall, kind
Karen's grandmother: Catherine Lewis, 65, English, short, kind

Listening p. 25

Script

Hi. I am Jonathan. This is a picture of my family. The woman is my wife, Catherine. She is nice and thin. I have a son and a daughter, too. My daughter's name is Nancy. She is very smart. My son Kevin is outgoing. He loves soccer.

A

1. Catherine 2. Jonathan 3. Nancy
4. Kevin

B

nice, smart, outgoing

C

1. c 2. a 3. c

Who is this?

Listening p. 27

Script

1. This is my friend. Her name is Sarah. She is 23 years old. She is a student.
2. My friend's name is John. He's 19 years old.
3. This is my friend. He is 25 years old. He's from Japan. He lives in Tokyo.

A

1. a 2. a 3. c

Script

Hi. My name is Tim. I have many friends. My friend Kevin is a baseball player. He is very strong and tall. Karen is my classmate. She is 18 years old and likes painting. David is my classmate, too. He is American. He is 19 years old. He likes reading. Tommy is my best friend. He is smart and kind. He works at a restaurant.

B

1. Kevin 2. Karen 3. David
4. Tommy

C

1. He is a baseball player.
2. She is 18 years old.
3. He is American.
4. No, he isn't.
5. Tommy works at a restaurant.

People I Know

Reading p. 28

Comprehension Check

1. Ryan is smart.
2. No, he is tall.
3. She is from Australia.
4. No, she likes blouses and skirts.
5. She is 33 years old.

Vocabulary p. 28

A

1. red 2. green 3. yellow
4. orange 5. gray 6. black

B

1. glasses 2. T-shirt 3. blue jeans
4. earrings 5. skirt 6. necklace
7. cap 8. blouse 9. shorts

Wrap-up p. 30

B

Appearances: tall, thin, pretty, young

Personalities: outgoing, kind, shy, talkative

Unit 3 Things

Warm-up p. 31

A

1. pen 2. computer 3. desk
4. bag 5. wallet 6. key

What's in your bag?

Vocabulary p. 32

* There are NO glasses in this picture.

Listening p. 32

Script

A: Wow. You have a dirty desk, Pierre.
B: It's okay. I know where everything is . . .
A: Really? Then where is your watch?
B: It's here.
A: Do you have a USB drive?
B: Yes. I have one . . . here.
A: And your glasses?
B: Hmm . . . Interesting. I know they are around here somewhere.
A: They are on your face.
B: That's right.

A

1. a 2. b

B

1. True
2. False

Grammar p. 33

B

1. an
2. brothers
3. horses
4. boxes
5. a
6. a
7. boys
8. bears
9. students
10. car

What is this?

Listening p. 35

Script

A: How do you like the room?

B: It's very nice. I like it.

A: This is my bed, so that is yours.

B: Cool.

A: You can use those bookshelves over there. Oh, here. These are the keys to the house.

B: Thanks.

B

1. b
2. c
3. a

Which one is it?

Listening p. 37

Script

A: I really like that purple bag on the top shelf.

B: It's not bad. But I like the green one under the hats better.

A: Hmm . . . I don't know. I don't like green.

B: How about the dark blue bag by the table?

A: The small one? It's actually cute. I like it.

B: Do you want to go in and ask the price?

A: Sure. Wait. Where is my little sister?

B: Turn around. She is right behind you.

B

1. c
2. c

I am messy.

Reading p. 39

Comprehension Check

1. James is messy.
2. Alex is clean.
3. because James doesn't clean his room
4. There are two beds and two desks.
5. He wants to be clean.

Wrap-up p. 40

B

an apple	apples
a shoe	shoes
a bus	buses
an eraser	erasers

C

1. This
2. That
3. Those
4. These

D

1. on
2. by
3. on

Unit 4 Daily Life

Warm-up p. 41

A

1. date
2. month
3. day
4. year
5. time
6. week

My show is on.

TV Schedule p. 42

1. It starts at 8:00 p.m.
2. It's on Channel 05.
3. It starts at 9:00 p.m.
4. *Three Sisters* is on.
5. It ends at 9:00 p.m.

Vocabulary p. 43

B

1. three o'clock
2. a quarter to five
3. 5:50
4. 4:30

Listening p. 43

Script

1. A: What time is it?
   B: It's half past ten.
2. A: When does the movie start?
   B: It starts at a quarter past eight.
3. A: When does the class finish?
   B: It finishes at twenty to three.
4. A: When is lunch?
   B: Lunch is at noon.

1. 10:30
2. 8:15
3. 2:40
4. 12:00

I get up at 7 o'clock.

Grammar p. 44

B

1. eat 2. doesn't leave 3. take
4. has 5. go 6. don't watch
7. Do, go

Reading p. 45

Comprehension Check

1. Yes, she does.
2. Sam does.
3. He studies Chinese.
4.

Friday	Janice	Sam
Morning	She goes to school.	He drinks coffee.
Afternoon	She meets her friends at a coffee shop.	He goes for a walk.
Evening	She watches TV.	He works at a bar.

How's your sister?

Vocabulary p. 46

C

Grammar p. 47

B

1. in 2. in 3. on
4. at 5. in 6. on

Listening p. 47

Script

A: John, do you want to come to my birthday party?
B: Sure. When is it, Mika?
A: It's on March 2nd at seven o'clock.
B: Where is it?
A: It's at Tony's Pizzeria.
B: That sounds great!

B

1. False 2. False

I never take the bus.

Reading p. 48

Comprehension Check

1. She always wakes up at 6 a.m.
2. She never takes the bus to work.
3. She sometimes buys bread.
4. She rarely watches TV.

Wrap-up p. 50

A

1. o'clock 2. fifteen 3. ten, ten
4. half, five

B

1. get up 2. takes 3. doesn't go

D

1. She rarely gets up late.
2. She always does the dishes.
3. She sometimes drives to work.
4. She never exercises.

Unit 5 Pastimes and Weekends

Warm-up p. 51

A

basketball, fishing, baseball, yoga, skiing

What do you do on the weekend?

Grammar p. 52

B

1. plays 2. do 3. go
4. go 5. plays 6. does

Listening p. 53

Script

A: Caroline, what do you do when you have a day off?
B: I like to go jogging with my husband. How about you, Ted?
A: I usually take my dog for a walk at the park.
B: That's nice.

A

1. b 2. c

B

1. True 2. False 3. False

What do you do for fun?

Grammar p. 54

B

1. When 2. When 3. Who
4. Where 5. Who

Listening p. 55

Script
1. A: What do you do for fun, Chen?
B: I go swimming.
A: When do you go swimming?
B: I go swimming on Saturday morning.
2. A: Yui, what is your hobby?
B: I play board games with my family.
A: Where do you usually play?
B: We usually play at my grandparents' house.
3. A: Matt, what do you do on the weekend?
B: I go fishing with my dad.
A: Why do you go fishing?
B: Because it is very relaxing.

1. a 2. c 3. c

What do you do on the weekend when it's sunny?

Vocabulary p. 56

1. rainy 2. stormy 3. windy
4. snowy 5. spring 6. summer
7. winter

Grammar p. 57

B

1. When do you do aerobics
2. when it is rainy
3. When I have a day off
4. When do you go for a walk

Listening p. 57

Script
A: The summer is really hot. I hate it. What do you think, Alex?
B: I like the summer.
A: Really? What do you think about the winter?
B: I hate the winter. It's too cold.
A: Well, what about the spring?
B: I don't like the spring. It's too rainy. I love the fall. The weather is really nice in the fall.

1. winter, cold 2. doesn't like

My Day Off

Reading p. 58

A

Comprehension Check
1. He is a businessman.
2. He plays golf with his boss.
3. He goes to the tennis club.
4. He goes to the supermarket after lunch.
5. He cooks dinner for his family. He plays board games with them.
6. They go to bed at 10:00 p.m.
7. He goes to sleep at 12:00 a.m.

Wrap-up p. 60

A

1. go jogging
2. does yoga
3. plays tennis

B

1. b 2. d 3. e
4. a 5. c

C

1. winter 2. summer 3. fall
4. spring

D

1. She goes skiing in the winter.
2. She goes for walks with her husband.
3. She gets home from work at 5:30 p.m.
4. She goes to sleep at 10:30 p.m.

Unit 6 Directions

Warm-up p. 61

A

1. bakery 2. coffee shop 3. pizzeria
4. drugstore 5. clothes shop 6. flower shop

B

1. clothes shop 2. drugstore 3. pizzeria
4. flower shop

Where are you?

Listening p. 62

Script
A: Marcia, I am on the 2nd floor. Where are you?

B: I'm in the clothes shop. I want to buy a new dress.
A: The clothes shop? Where's that?
B: It's between the coffee shop and the bakery.
A: Oh, okay. I see it now.

A
bakery, coffee shop, clothes shop

B
1. b 2. a 3. c

Grammar p. 62

B
1. on the corner of 2. next to 3. on, in
4. across from 5. between

I live on Green Street.

Conversation p. 63

B
1. They live on Green Street.
2. c
3. b
4. She works at the hospital.

How do I get to the park?

Listening p. 64

Script
A: Excuse me, sir. How do I get to the post office?
B: It's right next to the school.
A: Um . . . Where is the school? I don't live around here.
B: Go straight on 1st Street. The post office is across from the police station.

A
1. False 2. True 3. False

B
1

City Map p. 65

A
Jennifer – bank
Lauren – movie theater
Mike – police station
Juan – train station

B
1. library 2. bank 3. hospital

Around Town

Megan's Neighborhood p. 66

Script
Every Monday morning, I'm very busy. First, I take my kids to school. Next, I go to the library to return some books. Then, I usually go to the bank and the grocery store. After that, I go home and get some rest.

A
1. a
2.

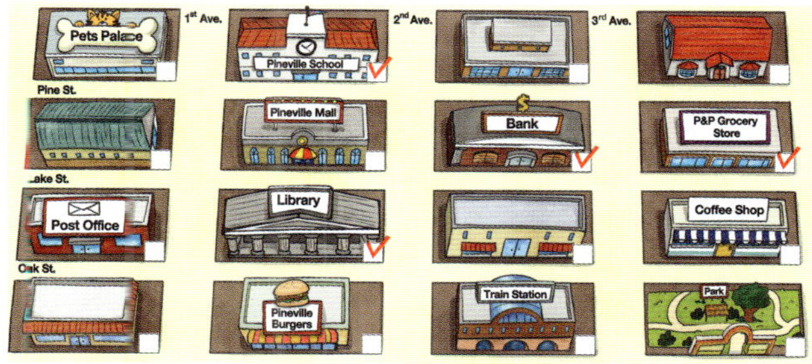

Script
I am Samantha. My sister Megan is sick today. She needs my help. Right now, I am on the corner of 2nd Avenue and Pine Street. I need to pick up my two nieces. Then, we want to go to the burger place. People say Pineville Burgers makes really good cheeseburgers. But how do I get there?

B
1.

2. b

C
1.

2. b

Popular Places to Visit

Reading p. 68

Comprehension Check

1. Ripley's Museum is popular with adults and children.
2. It has many scary and surprising things.
3. Children don't pay.
4. Pier 39 has nice restaurants and street performances.
5. There is a magic show.
6. Free shows are on Fridays.

Wrap-up p. 70

A

1. on, in 2. between 3. next to

B

1st Street, Turn left, Turn right, the corner

Unit 7 Shopping

Warm-up p. 71

A

1. bakery 2. flower shop 3. coffee shop
4. clothes shop

B

1. a clothes shop 2. a coffee shop 3. a bakery
4. a flower shop

How much is this umbrella?

Listening p. 73

Script

1. A: How much are these earrings?
   B: They are $70.46.
   A: $17.46? Here is $20.00
   B: No, they are $70.46.
2. A: How much is this ring?
   B: It's $49.99.
   A: Okay. I'll take it.
3. A: What are these?
   B: They're necklaces.
   A: How much are they?
   B: They're $18.50 each.
4. A: Is this watch expensive?
   B: No, it's only $14.80.
   A: That's cheap.

1. b 2. a 3. b
4. b

Vocabulary p. 73

B

1. checks 2. credit cards 3. cash
4. coin

They are in the Electronics Department.

Vocabulary p. 74

A

Electronics: 1, 8
Clothing & Shoes: 6, 3
Home Appliances: 5, 7
Health & Beauty: 2, 4

B

1. Clothing Department
2. Home Appliances Department
3. Shoes

I'd like to exchange this shirt.

Grammar p. 76

B

1. This shirt is too small.
2. This car is so fast.
3. This bag is too expensive.

I want to return it.

Listening p. 77

Script

1. A: I'd like to return this jacket.
   B: What's the matter with it?
   A: It's too expensive.
   B: Do you have the receipt?
   A: It's right here.
2. A: I'd like to return these pants.
   B: What's the problem?
   A: I don't like the style.
   B: I see.
3. A: This dress is too long. I would like to exchange it.
   B: Do you have the receipt?
   A: Yes. Here it is.
   B: Thank you.

1. return, expensive
2. return, style
3. exchange, short

Shopping Habits

Reading p. 78

Comprehension Check

1. They have different shopping habits.
2. Kathy loves to go shopping at department stores and malls. Ken likes shopping online.
3. He likes shopping online because it is cheaper and people deliver the packages to his house.
4. Shopping online is easier, but sometimes the clothes don't fit.
5. The couple needs to find something they both like doing.

Listening p. 79

Script

Hi. I am Patty. I want to talk about the Rainbow Café. It is right next to my work. The café is small, but it sells the best coffee and muffins. Their cheesecake muffins are my favorite. I go there every morning before work.

My name is Janet. My favorite place is Fashion House. It is an online shop. It has beautiful dresses and cool shoes. But its clothes are a little expensive, so I only shop there when there is a sale.

My name is Mindy. I think the Don't Pay More Bookstore is the best bookstore. It is next to the church I go to. I buy all my books there. It has lots and lots of books. And its books are usually cheaper. I go there every Sunday.

A

1. Janet
2. Patty
3. Mindy

B

1. a
2. c
3. c
4. b.
5. c

Wrap-up p. 80

B

1. headphones
2. Pharmacy & Health
3. Home Appliances
4. blue jeans

C

1. exchange, small
2. return, expensive

Unit 8 Food

Warm-up p. 81

A

B

1. tomatoes
2. apples
3. bread
4. cheese
5. beef

Is there any milk in the refrigerator?

Grammar p. 82

B

1. any
2. some
3. some
4. any, any
5. any, any
6. some
7. some, some
8. any

Listening p. 83

Script

A: I'm hungry. Do we have any potato chips?

B: I think there are some in the cupboard.

A: Really? I don't see them.

B: Then eat some yogurt instead.

A: Where's the yogurt?

B: It's in the refrigerator. It's on the top shelf in front of the orange juice.

A: I see it. Thanks.

A

1. a
2. b

B

1. True
2. False
3. True
4. False

I need a box of cereal.

Listening p. 84

Script

A: So what do we need?

B: We need some cans of tuna fish.

A: Tuna is over there. Three cans?

B: Yep. Next, let's buy a dozen eggs.

A: Okay.

B: We need a bag of rice, too.

A: Large or small?

B: A small bag.

A: So what's for dinner?

B: Pork chops with fried rice.

A: Sounds good. Do we need some pork?

B: No, we have some at home.

A: Before we line up, I'd like to get a bottle of diet soda.

B: Okay, hurry up!

A

1. b   2. c

B

three cans of tuna fish

twelve eggs

a bag of rice

Reading p. 85

Comprehension Check

1. He eats fast food.
2. It is cheap and delicious.
3. She thinks it is a bad idea.
4. She wants to cook beef stew.
5. He needs to buy some potatoes, onions, and carrots.

I'd like to order a hamburger.

Listening p. 86

Script

A: Welcome to Burger House. How can I help you?

B: Yes, I'd like to order three hamburgers, two French fries, one soda, and four chocolate shakes . . .

A: Anything else?

B: No, that's it. Um, actually, one small salad, please.

A: Okay. That'll be $25.97.

B: I'm sorry. How much?

A: $25.97. Pay at the next window.

B: Okay.

A: Thank you. Come again!

A

1, 3, 5, 6, 9

B

1. c   2. a

I'd like the chicken lunch, please.

Listening p. 87

Script

Today's special is the fish sandwich. It comes with your choice of the following soups: chicken noodle, tomato basil, or clam chowder. It also comes with a drink. We have soda, iced tea, and coffee.

A

Fish sandwich

Script

1. A: I would like one ham sandwich and a can of soda.
   B: Sure.
2. A: Can I have the mushroom soup and a glass of orange juice?
   B: I'm sorry. We don't have any orange juice.
   A: I see. Just the soup, please.
3. A: The tomato basil soup and a cup of Americano, please.
   B: Sure. Is that all?
   A: Yes. Thanks.

B

1. Ham sandwich   2. Mushroom soup   3. Americano

A Recipe for Weekday Super Pizza

Reading p. 88

A

Comprehension Check

1. cooking   2. pizza   3. 4
4. 220   5. bake

B

First, ham, mozzarella cheese, pineapple, Finally

Writing p. 89

A

1.

Wrap-up p. 90

A

1. any, some 2. any, any 3. some, any

B

1. There is some cheese.
2. There is a bottle of wine.
3. There is a bag of chips.
4. There is some meat.
5. There are some bananas.

Unit 9 Body and Health

Warm-up p. 91

1. eye 2. mouth 3. nose
4. tooth/teeth 5. neck 6. shoulder
7. hair 8. knee 9. ankle
10. hip 11. back 12. arm
13. finger 14. toe 15. foot/feet

I am just resting.

Vocabulary p. 92

B

1. runny nose 2. fever 3. toothache
4. sore throat 5. cold 6. headache

Grammar p. 93

B

1. is watching 2. are eating
3. am not studying 4. are listening
5. I'm not, am playing 6. isn't swimming
7. is raining

Listening p. 93

Script

A: Hey, Dad.
B: Mandy, how are you?
A: I'm not doing so well. I have a really bad toothache.
B: I'm sorry, honey.

A: Jake, what are you doing?
B: I'm drinking some hot tea.
A: Tea? You hate drinking tea.
B: Yeah, but it's good for my sore throat.

A

1. False 2. True 3. True
4. False

Script

1. A: Hello? Hello?
   B: Hello.
   A: What's wrong? You don't sound good.
   B: I think I have the flu.
   A: Oh, that's not good.
   B: Let's talk later. I'm going back home right now. I need a rest.
2. A: What's the matter?
   B: My left leg hurts. It's really bad.
   A: Why don't you go see a doctor?
   B: I'm in the doctor's office now. I'm waiting for Dr. Greene.

B

1. a. the flu b. home
2. a. leg b. waiting for

I feel terrible.

Grammar p. 94

B

1. Don't eat 2. Don't smoke 3. Don't stay up
4. Exercise 5. Spend 6. Be

Listening p. 95

Script

1. A: Hello, Sarah. What's the problem?
   B: I have a sore throat.
   A: Oh, that's too bad. Drink some lemon tea with honey.
2. A: What's the problem, Chen?
   B: My back hurts. It's killing me.
   A: I think you sit for too long. Take a break. Walk around the office during the day.
3. A: What's the matter, James?
   B: I have a stomachache.
   A: Take these pills.
4. A: What's wrong, Amanda?
   B: I have a fever, a cough, and a really bad headache.
   A: I think you have the flu. Take this medicine and rest at home

A

1. a sore throat 2. a backache 3. a stomachache
4. the flu

Script

A: Lynn, for a cold, first, take these pills.
B: Thanks. Anything else?
A: Drink more liquids. When I say liquids, I mean water, not coffee, tea, or alcohol.
B: I got it.

A: And stay in bed and be lazy. Don't try to do too much. Listen to your body. If it wants to sleep all day, do it.

B: Okay, thanks.

B

1. Do
2. Don't
3. Do
4. Do

This is my usual breakfast.

Listening p. 96

Script

Hello. I am Dr. Barns. Today, I want to tell you about three healthy habits. First, eat well. Eating too much, eating too little, and eating too late at night are all bad for you. Eat, at least three times a day, with lots of vegetables and fruits. And don't forget to drink enough water. Second, exercise. If you are too busy, then try to walk more. Use the stairs instead of the elevator. Easy, right? Leave your car at home once a week. That's a start. Third, think positively. This is very important. Look into the mirror and say, "You are doing fine." Believe it or not, this is a magic sentence.

A

3, 4, 5, 7

B

1. c
2. b

Listening p. 97

Script

A: Tom, is that you?

B: Oh, hey, Angela.

A: What are you doing these days? You look great!

B: Thanks. I am trying to be healthy. I'm running almost every day and doing yoga three times a week.

A: Wow. That is amazing.

B: And I am not eating snacks too late at night.

A: Keep it up. You look amazing!

B: Thanks!

A

1. True
2. False

B

1. a
2. a, c
3. b

Old but Healthy

Reading p. 98

Comprehension Check

1. She is 102 years old.
2. Gardening is important to her.
3. She lives with her granddaughter.
4. She visits her friends once or twice a month.
5. She enjoys outdoor activities, eats well, stays close to her family and friends, and tries to think positively.

Wrap-up p. 100

A

1. is touching, headache
2. is holding, runny nose
3. is coughing, cold

B

1. Don't stay up
2. Eat
3. Drink
4. Don't drink
5. Don't smoke

C

1. She goes to school five times a week.
2. She watches movies once a week.
3. She does aerobics three times a week.
4. She eats at a restaurant twice a week.

Unit 10 Work and Jobs

Can you cook?

Grammar p. 102

B

1. can't
2. can
3. Can
4. can't
5. can
6. Can
7. can't
8. can

Listening p. 103

Script

A: Hey, Benjamin, do you want to go skiing with Allen and me this weekend?

B: Sure. But I can't ski very well. I fall down all the time.

A: Don't worry. Allen can teach you.

B: Really? Then I want to go!

A

1. a
2. c

Script

A: Hey, Benjamin. How's it going?

B: It's okay, I guess. I can't do much with just one arm. I can't cook or play computer games. But I can type very slowly.

A: How do you get to work?

B: I walk. I can't ride a bike now because I can't use both hands.

A: That's too bad. Do you need a ride? I can drive you to work.

B: Thanks, but that's okay. I can walk.

A: All right. I'm really sorry you're hurt. I hope you get better soon.

B: Thanks.

B

type, walk to work

How well can you do it? p. 103

B

1. can't, at all
2. can, a little
3. can, very well

Is doing an internship good or bad?

Reading p. 104

Comprehension Check

1. b. Interns can meet lots of people in the industry.
   c. Interns can make their résumés stronger.
2. b. Interns sometimes can't make any money for their work.
   c. At the ends of the internships, companies tell their interns they can't hire them.

Listening p. 104

Script

A: How's it going with your internship, Lily?

B: I like it. I am learning a lot and meeting new people.

A: Yeah? That's good to hear.

B: I know. What are you up to, Erin?

A: I am actually going to the Cameron Insurance Company right now.

B: Huh? Why?

A: For a job interview. It's hiring some students for typing or something.

B: Typing? You hate boring work.

A: Yes, I do. But at least I can make $15 per hour.

1. True 2. False 3. True
4. True 5. False

Looking for a Job

Reading p. 105

B

1. construction work
2. $20
3. cleaning work
4. She needs to call Simon.
5. fruit-picking work
6. He needs to call 0489-564-4390.

I want a job.

Listening p. 106

Script

A: Samuel, can you look at my application form? I'm applying for a part-time job.

B: Sure. Let me see . . . You are applying for an assistant manager position, huh?

A: Yes, I am. My major is business, you know. So I think it's a good opportunity. I can get experience. Maybe even a full-time job in the future.

B: Well, that is a good idea. But I don't think this is a good idea.

A: What do you mean?

B: Look here. Do you really want to work 16 hours a day?

A: No, of course not! That's a mistake. I want to work 16 hours a week.

B: Then change it. Everything else looks good, by the way.

A

1. c 2. b 3. a
4. b

Script

I think I look better in these clothes. Okay. Let's try it again. First, I want to say thank you very much for having me today. My name is Jane Lynn Kelly. I am a senior at Cardenas College. I am majoring in science technology . . . I don't have any office experience, but I am ready to learn. I'm a hardworking, diligent, and motivated person . . . I enjoy reading books. So every Sunday, I read books for the children at National Hospital.

B

1. Jane 2. science technology
3. Hardworking 4. Reading books
5. hospital

Speaking p. 107

Q1. What are your strengths

Q2. Can you tell me about your education

Q3. Can you work on holidays and weekends

Q4. What are your hobbies

Q5. When can you start

Opportunities Abroad

Reading p. 108

A

Comprehension Check

1. He is working at a vineyard.
2. He wakes up at 5 a.m.
3. He can have a day off when it rains.
4. He thinks it is okay because he can make good money.
5. It shows three.
6. It is the internship opportunity in Mexico.

B

1. They are looking for healthy and strong volunteers.
2. They can dig wells for fresh drinking water.
   They can help build houses.

Listening p. 109

Script

1. A: Mom, I have good news.
   B: What is it, Julia?
   A: It's an internship. I can work with real architects.
   B: Really? How exciting.
   A: I know. But it's in Portugal. So I can't come home during the summer.
   B: Oh, no.
2. A: Let's go to Myanmar right now. The people there need our help.
   B: I don't know, Dan. It's dangerous there, isn't it? Besides, we don't have any money. Where do we stay?
   A: Don't worry. The volunteer program can give us food and a place to stay.
   B: I don't know. I can't work for free. I want to save some money and buy a car.
3. A: Hi. Is this Dominic?
   B: Yes, it is. Who's calling?
   A: My name's Lucy. I'm calling about the study abroad program in England. I have a question.
   B: Sure. What would you like to know?
   A: I really want to travel around Europe. Are there any breaks?
   B: Well, there's a two-week break in April. Lots of students travel around Europe by train then.
   A: That's great. Thank you.

A

1. Lucy 2. Dan 3. Julia

B

1. architects 2. cannot 3. can't
4. travel 5. two-week

Wrap-up p. 110

A

1. Brook can play sports.
2. Brook can't use a computer.
3. Brook can cook.
4. Brook can speak French.
5. Brook can't dance.

B

Doing an internship is a good idea.	Internships are a waste of time.
Ada, Eunmi	Cory, Rana

C

1. Halim 2. Jakarta State 3. Biology
4. good listener 5. playing soccer

Unit 11 Experience

Warm-up p. 111

1. Marilyn 2. A. J. 3. Li Wei
4. Danny 5. Hana

You were so cute.

Grammar p. 112

B

1. was 2. Were, wasn't 3. weren't

C

1. It was sunny
2. Jack and Jill were 9 years old
3. I was tired
4. You were upset

Listening p. 113

Script

A: I love our new apartment! It's big, new, and bright.
B: Quite cheap, too!
A: I know! Our old place was a bit . . .
B: What? Small, old, and dark?
A: Yes, and smelly.
B: I agree. The carpet was difficult to clean. It was disgusting.
A: And our neighbors weren't really nice to us.
B: No, they were very rude.
A: I'm happy that we live here now.
B: Me, too.
Bang! Bang! Bang!
C: OKAY, WE ARE ALL HAPPY. NOW BE QUIET!

A

1. new 2. bright 3. smelly
4. nice 5. happy

B

old, difficult, nice, cheap, smelly, disgusting

Did you do anything fun?

Grammar p. 114

B

1. stayed 2. danced 3. stopped

4. did, arrive

C

1. I visited my grandparents
2. Did Carrie work at a department store
3. The photographers didn't follow the wolves
4. We checked our email

Listening p. 115

Script

A: Leave me a message after the beep.

B: Hey, Georgia. I guess you aren't home. I'm back, and I'm very tired. My trip wasn't great. Actually, it was terrible. I didn't hear my alarm in the morning. I almost missed my plane. My seat on the plane was between two big guys. The hotel was old and dirty. It didn't look anything like the pictures on the Internet. I even lost my camera. I wasted my time and money!

A

1. True
2. False
3. False
4. True

Script

A: Hello. Mr. Simon?

B: Yes, speaking.

A: This is Jennifer from the Hilltop Hotel. I believe we have your camera.

B: Really?

A: Yes, sir. Is it correct that you stayed in Room 321 on May 28th?

B: Yes.

A: And you stayed with us for 4 nights. Correct?

B: Yes. That's correct.

A: After you checked out, we discovered a silver camera behind the sofa.

B: Does it have a red strap?

A: Yes, it does.

B: That's my camera!

B

1. 321
2. 4
3. camera
4. red

What happened yesterday?

Vocabulary p. 116

1. do the laundry
2. spend time online
3. make food
4. take a shower
5. do the dishes
6. call a friend
7. see someone
8. sleep

Grammar p. 117

B

1. had
2. Did, do
3. put

C

1. My mom drank a cup of coffee
2. The farmer went to bed early
3. Veronica read two books

Listening p. 117

Script

A: So?

B: Carlos took me to a nice restaurant near the town hall. He ordered some steaks and wine for us.

A: Wine?

B: Yes. We ate and drank. We had a wonderful time. Suddenly, he held my hand and smiled.

A: Oh, my goodness. You're kidding!

B: Then he said, "Maria, my darling, please pay for dinner. I forgot to bring my wallet."

A: What?

B: I spent more than $300 on dinner last night.

B

1. a restaurant
2. wine
3. his wallet

Learning Vacation Reviews

Reading p. 118

Comprehension Check

1. He went to France.
2. Pierre taught Allen how to make wine.
3. He began learning the same day he arrived.
4. She wanted to learn to scuba dive.
5. She didn't have a teacher when she arrived. When the teacher came, he didn't speak English.

Listening p. 119

Script

1. My parents and I went to Morocco last year. It was really hot, but it was really beautiful. We rode camels and went to a market at night. We ate good food. I took lots of pictures. It was a great trip. So I want to give it 5 stars.
2. I was in London for a week last month. I didn't like the city very much. It was too crowded and dirty. The weather was cold and cloudy. But London Bridge was interesting. So I give it two stars.

A

1. a
2. b

B

1. False 2. True 3. True
4. False 5. False 6. True

Wrap-up p. 120

B

1. was 2. weren't 3. wasn't
4. Were

C

1. Did, see, worked
2. Did, go, did, gave, Did, take, took
3. Did, enjoy, ate

Unit 12 Plans

Warm-up p. 121

1. He is going to have a sales meeting on Monday.
2. Ken and Karen are going to get married.
3. He is going to go on a business trip for 3 days.
4. He is going to go fishing on the 14th and 15th of June.
5. He is going to have tennis lessons 3 times in June.

Weekend Plans

Grammar p. 122

B

1. is going to visit 2. am going to call
3. will take, won't be 4. aren't going to take
5. will have 6. am going to graduate
7. is she going to meet 8. Are they going to play

Listening p. 123

Script

A: Do you have any plans for the weekend, Tommy?

B: I'm going to be really busy. On Saturday morning, I'm going to take my children to the amusement park. After that, we are going to visit my wife's parents. Then, I'm going to clean the garage on Sunday morning and wash my car in the afternoon.

A: Wow, that is a busy weekend.

B: What about you, Suzy?

A: I'm going to see a movie on Saturday night.

B: And Sunday?

A: I'm going to sleep in. That's all.

A

1. d 2. c

B

1. a 2. c. 3. b
4. c

Over the Holidays

Listening p. 125

Script

A: Hey, Alex. What are you going to do over the holiday?

B: Actually, I'm going to take these reports home and finish them over the holiday.

A: Are you kidding me? Why don't you go skiing with us? My family and I are going to go to Brown Bear Mountain. It's a great ski resort.

B: I'd love to, but I can't. My boss will be angry with me. I really need to finish them.

A: Okay. Maybe next time.

A

1. True 2. False 3. True

Script

A: Hold on just a second, Ben. When are you going to leave for Brown Bear Mountain?

B: We are going to leave the day after tomorrow on Saturday.

A: How are you going to get there?

B: We're going to take my van. There's lots of space.

A: What time are you going to leave?

B: Bright and early at 6 a.m.

A: Are you sure you have room for one more?

B: Of course, Alex.

A: Okay. I will see you on Saturday.

B

1. b 2. c 3. a
4. b

Inviting and Accepting/Declining an Invitation

Listening p. 127

Script

A: Who is going to come to our party this Friday night?

B: Let me check my email . . . Lola says sorry, but she can't come. She says she is going to be on a vacation.

A: Okay.

B: Santiago is going to come . . . but late.

A: He always comes late. What about Minju? Any messages from her?

B: Here is her email. She says . . . no. She doesn't feel well. She is going to stay home.

A: Oh, that's not good. And your brothers, Chris and Carl?

B: They are not going to come to our party.

A: Really? I thought they wanted to come.

B: They will make a mess. So I didn't tell them about the party.

A: So it's just going to be you, Santiago, and me?
B: Pretty much.

A

1. a 2. b

B

1. a 2. c

Unusual Tours

Reading p. 128

Comprehension Check

1. The Creepy Hollywood Bus Tour is in Los Angeles.
2. It is Hobbiton.
3. The tour is very popular.
4. It costs one million dollars.
5. They're going to float, look at the earth, and eat real astronaut food.

Listening p. 129

Script

A: You lived in New York City before, right?
B: Yeah, in 2015. Why?
A: Where in the city did you live? I'd like to go there.
B: Are you going to go to New York?
A: Yeah. Next week. It's for a business trip, but I'd like to do some sightseeing.
B: I lived in Dumbo near the Manhattan Bridge. Where are you going to stay?
A: In a hotel near Chinatown.
B: Well, you can take the subway to get there.
A: Okay.
B: Or you can walk across the Brooklyn Bridge.
A: Really? That sounds fun. I am going to walk across the Brooklyn Bridge then!

A

1. week 2. business 3. Dumbo
4. on foot

Script

Let me tell you a bit about what we are going to do for the next 4 hours. First, we are going to take the ferry to Liberty Island. On the way there, you can learn the history of the island. Once we get there, we are going to go inside the base of the Statue of Liberty. We are going to go to the museum there and then go up to the observation deck. After that, we are going to take the ferry to Ellis Island. There, we are going to have some free time. You can explore the island and visit the museum.

B

1, We are going to take the ferry to Liberty Island.
4, We are going to have free time on Ellis Island.
2, We are going to go to the museum in the Statue of Liberty.
3, We are going to go up to the observation deck.

Wrap-up p. 130

A

1. won't go
2. are going to go
3. Is, going to call
4. Will, take, will call
5. are, going to do, They're going to travel

B

1. d 2. b 3. a
4. c

List of Irregular Verbs

Infinitive	Past Simple	Past Participle
be	was/were	been
beat	beat	beaten
begin	began	begun
bend	bent	bent
bet	bet	bet
bind	bound	bound
bite	bit	bitten
blow	blew	blown
break	broke	broken
bring	brought	brought
broadcast	broadcast	broadcast
build	built	built
buy	bought	bought
catch	caught	caught
choose	chose	chosen
come	came	come
cost	cost	cost
cut	cut	cut
deal	dealt	dealt
dig	dug	dug
do	did	done
draw	drew	drawn
drink	drank	drunk
drive	drove	driven
eat	ate	eaten
fall	fell	fallen
feed	fed	fed
feel	felt	felt
fight	fought	fought
find	found	found
fly	flew	flown
forget	forgot	forgotten
freeze	froze	frozen
get	got	gotten
give	gave	given
go	went	gone
grow	grew	grown
hang	hung	hung
have	had	had
hear	heard	heard
hide	hid	hidden
hit	hit	hit
hold	held	held
hurt	hurt	hurt
keep	kept	kept
know	knew	known
lay	laid	laid
lead	led	led
leave	left	left
lend	lent	lent
let	let	let
lie	lay	lain
lose	lost	lost

Infinitive	Past Simple	Past Participle
make	made	made
mean	meant	meant
meet	met	met
pay	paid	paid
put	put	put
read	read*	read*
ride	rode	ridden
ring	rang	rung
rise	rose	risen
run	ran	run
say	said	said
see	saw	seen
sell	sold	sold
send	sent	sent
set	set	set
shake	shook	shaken
shine	shone	shone
shoot	shot	shot
show	showed	shown
shrink	shrank	shrunk
shut	shut	shut
sing	sang	sung
sink	sank	sunk
sit	sat	sat
sleep	slept	slept
slide	slid	slid
speak	spoke	spoken
speed	sped	sped
spend	spent	spent
spin	spun	spun
spit	spat	spat
split	split	split
spread	spread	spread
spring	sprang	sprung
stand	stood	stood
steal	stole	stolen
stick	stuck	stuck
sting	stung	stung
stink	stank	stunk
strike	struck	struck
swear	swore	sworn
swim	swam	swum
swing	swung	swung
take	took	taken
teach	taught	taught
tear	tore	torn
tell	told	told
think	thought	thought
throw	threw	thrown
wake	woke	woken
wear	wore	worn
win	won	won
write	wrote	written

*pronounced [rɛd]

MEMO

MEMO